WRITTEN SKILLS FOR SQE2

QUESTIONS & ANSWERS IN

CRIMINAL LITIGATION

Philip Cowburn

Series editors: Amy and David Sixsmith

REVISE SQE

First published in 2026 by Fink Publishing Ltd

Impression number 10 9 8 7 6 5 4 3 2 1

British Library Cataloguing in Publication Data
A catalogue record for this book is available from the British Library
ISBN: 9781914213984

This book is also available in various ebook formats.
Ebook ISBN: 9781914213991

Cover and text design by BMLD (bmld.uk)
Production and typesetting by Westchester Publishing Services UK
Development editing by Llinos Edwards
Academic consulting by Mark Thomas

Fink Publishing Ltd
E-mail: hello@revise4law.co.uk
www.revise4law.co.uk

Acknowledgements
The author and publisher would like to thank the following copyright holders for their kind permission to reproduce material in this book:
RELX (UK) Limited, trading as LexisNexis: *Halsbury's Laws of England*, p. 33.
Extracts from the SRA website in this book are owned by and published under licence from the Solicitors Regulation Authority of The Cube, 199 Wharfside Street, Birmingham, B1 1RN, which asserts its right to be identified as the author of this work in accordance with the Copyright, Designs and Patents Act 1988 Sections 77 and 78: www.sra.org.uk/solicitors/standards-regulations/financial-services-conduct-business-rules/. Please refer to the SRA website to ensure you are relying upon the correct version and most up to date version of the Standards.
Every effort has been made to obtain necessary permission with reference to copyright material. The publishers apologise if inadvertently any sources remain unacknowledged and will gladly make suitable arrangements with any copyright holders whom it has not been possible to contact.

Notes from the publisher

1. This book reflects the SQE2 assessment specification (updated May 2026), applicable for assessments from 1 September 2026.
2. While Fink Publishing has made every attempt to ensure that advice on the qualification and its assessment is accurate, the official specification and associated assessment guidance materials are the only authoritative source of information and should always be referred to for definitive guidance. See the SRA website at https://sqe.sra.org.uk. Note that the SRA may amend their assessment guidance (including the contents of the assessment specifications) at any point.
3. Fink Publishing has robust editorial processes to ensure the accuracy of the content in this publication, and every effort is made to ensure this publication is free of errors. We are, however, only human, and occasionally errors do occur. Fink Publishing is not liable for any misunderstandings that arise as a result of errors in this publication, but it is our priority to ensure that the content is accurate. If you spot an error, please do contact us at **revise4law.co.uk** so we can make sure it is corrected.

Contents

Contributors	iv
Introduction	v
1 Case and matter analysis	1
Question 1	3
Sample answer 1 to question 1	7
Sample answer 2 to question 1	10
Question 2	12
Sample answer 1 to question 2	16
Sample answer 2 to question 2	19
2 Legal research	22
Question 1	24
Sample answer 1 to question 1	39
Sample answer 2 to question 1	41
Question 2	44
Sample answer 1 to question 2	63
Sample answer 2 to question 2	66
3 Legal writing	70
Question 1	72
Sample answer 1 to question 1	74
Sample answer 2 to question 1	77
Question 2	79
Sample answer 1 to question 2	81
Sample answer 2 to question 2	83
4 Legal drafting	86
Question 1	88
Sample answer 1 to question 1	93
Sample answer 2 to question 1	96
Question 2	98
Sample answer 1 to question 2	103
Sample answer 2 to question 2	106
Final words	109
Appendix	110
Performance indicators for SQE2 case and matter analysis assessment criteria	110
Performance indicators for SQE2 legal research assessment criteria	112
Performance indicators for SQE2 legal writing assessment criteria	114
Performance indicators for SQE2 legal drafting assessment criteria	116

Contributors

THE AUTHOR

Philip Cowburn is a practising criminal barrister, and former senior lecturer in law (fellow of Advance HE). At the bar, Philip prosecutes and defends in a wide range of criminal matters, spending much of his time in the Crown Court. Whilst in academia, Philip specialised in crime and professional discipline. Philip was assisted in drafting this text by Charlotte Paxford. Philip also extends his thanks to his instructing solicitors, some of whom have been consulted to ensure this text truly reflects practice at all levels in the criminal courts.

SERIES EDITORS

Dr Amy Sixsmith is associate professor in law at the University of Sunderland and a senior fellow of Advance HE.

Dr David Sixsmith is assistant professor in law at Northumbria Law School and a senior fellow of Advance HE.

Introduction

Welcome to *Revise SQE: Legal Skills for SQE2*! This series of revision guides is designed to support you through the second element of your Solicitors Qualifying Examination, in which you will be tested on your ability to put the legal knowledge you acquired for your SQE1 assessment into six different practical contexts.

The key to successfully navigating your SQE2 assessment can be split into three distinct areas:

- understanding how you are being assessed and what you are being assessed on
- practising example scenarios
- comparing and contrasting your answers with sample answers.

Our SQE2 guides are here to help you with this process, providing you not only with helpful guidance and top tips for approaching all of the relevant skills but also with multiple sample questions for each assessable skill in each of the relevant legal disciplines. Samples of high- and lower-scoring threshold answers to each question are provided, to guide you in good practice and steer you away from potential pitfalls.

Using this series in conjunction with our series of SQE1 revision guides for SQE1, to ensure that your legal knowledge is accurate and up to date, will enable you to tackle your SQE2 assessment with confidence.

PREPARING YOURSELF FOR SQE

The SQE is the route to qualification for aspiring solicitors and consists of two parts, as shown in this table.

Assessment	Contents of assessment
SQE1	• 360 multiple-choice questions • Closed book • Assessed over 2 sittings • Over 10 hours in total
SQE2	• Practical legal skills • 16 written and oral assessments • Assesses 6 practical legal skills • Over 14 hours in total

In addition to the above assessments, all candidates will have to undertake two years' qualifying work experience. More information on the SQE assessments can be found on the SRA website.

It is important to note that the SQE can be perceived to be a 'harder' set of assessments than the Legal Practice Course (LPC). The reason for this, explained by the SRA, is that the LPC is designed to prepare candidates for 'day one' of their training contract; the SQE, on the other hand, is designed to prepare candidates for 'day one' of being a newly qualified solicitor. With that in mind, and a different style of assessments in place, it is understandable that you might feel nervous or wary of the SQE.

This revision guide series will focus on preparation for SQE2. The SQE2 assessment is challenging as it asks candidates to put into practice the knowledge that they acquired for SQE1. This style of assessment is likely to be different from what you will have experienced before. We hope to alleviate some of those concerns, with guidance on preparing for the SQE assessment, tips on how to approach the skills-based assessments and detailed commentaries on sample answers to aid your revision.

WHAT DOES SQE2 ENTAIL?

SQE2 is split into two parts: oral and written. The table below shows the contexts in which these skills are assessed.

Part	Skills	Contexts
Oral	Client interview and attendance note/ legal analysis (hereafter referred to as 'interviewing')	Property practice Wills and intestacy, probate administration and practice
	Advocacy	Dispute resolution Criminal litigation
Written	Case and matter analysis Legal research Legal writing Legal drafting	Criminal litigation Dispute resolution Property practice Wills and intestacy, probate administration and practice Business organisations, rules and procedures

Oral skills

You will sit four oral skills examinations, which will take place over two half-days.

On day one you will be assessed in:

- advocacy in the context of dispute resolution
- interviewing in the context of property practice.

On day two you will be assessed in:

- advocacy in the context of criminal litigation
- interviewing in the context of wills and intestacy, probate administration and practice.

Written skills

For the written skills assessment, you will sit 12 examinations which will take place over three half-days. Every day you will be required to take an assessment in *each* of the written skills - legal research, case and matter analysis, legal writing and legal drafting.

On day one you will sit:
- two assessments in dispute resolution
- two assessments in criminal litigation.

On day two you will sit:
- two assessments in property practice
- two assessments in wills and intestacy, probate administration and practice.

On day three you will sit all four assessments in business organisations, rules and procedures.

HOW IS SQE2 MARKED?

Each of the SQE2 skills has its own set of assessment criteria. The *Revise SQE: Legal Skills for SQE2* series provides the following guidance:
- Oral skills – the criteria are outlined in ***Oral Skills for SQE2: Questions & Answers in Advocacy*** and examined in more depth in ***Oral Skills for SQE2: Client Interviewing and Negotiation*** and ***Oral Skills for SQE2: Advocacy***.
- Written skills – the criteria are outlined at the beginning of each chapter in our books covering the written skills for different legal contexts (see pages 2, 23, 71 and 87 in this text). The criteria are also explored in more detail in ***Introduction to Written Legal Skills for SQE2***.

The assessment is marked against the relevant criteria using the following scale:

A. Superior performance: well above the competency requirements of the assessment.
B. Clearly satisfactory: clearly meets the competency requirements of the assessment.
C. Marginal pass: on balance, just meets the competency requirements of the assessment.
D. Marginal fail: on balance, just fails to meet the competency requirements of the assessment.
E. Clearly unsatisfactory: clearly does not meet the competency requirements of the assessment.
F. Poor performance: well below the competency requirements of the assessment.

Your mark will be calculated by converting the grade into a numerical mark, with A representing 5 marks and F representing 0 marks.

The scaled scoring system

The SRA uses a scaled scoring system for all SQE2 assessments. This approach is designed to ensure that candidate scores are comparable across different assessment sittings, thereby providing a fair and consistent measure of candidate performance. The same system is in place for all SQE1 assessments.

The scaled scoring system works in the following way:
- Initially, candidates will receive a 'raw score' based on their performance across the 16 assessment stations in SQE2.
- A pass mark is then set for each assessment window. The pass mark is determined using statistical methods that account for any differences in question difficulty. This ensures fairness across different exam versions.
- Candidate raw scores are then converted to a common scale ranging from 0 to 500, with the pass mark consistently set at 300. This standardisation allows for direct comparisons between candidates' performances, regardless of the specific assessments they completed.

When you access your results, you will be able to see:

- a detailed breakdown of your results by assessment station (results will be expressed as marks from 0 to 5 for each assessment criterion across each of the 16 assessment stations)
- your overall mark expressed as a percentage
- your scaled score out of 500 – remember that the pass mark will always be set at 300.

For more information about the scaled scoring system, visit the SRA website.

It is very important that you are aware of the standard you are required to meet. The competence standard is that of a Day One Solicitor, which is mapped against Level 3 of the Threshold Standard for the Statement of Solicitor Competence. This is available on the SRA website, and we would encourage you to review this prior to sitting your SQE2 assessment.

The assessors

In terms of who will be assessing you against this standard and the relevant skills criteria, the interview will be marked by the person you are interviewing, while the remaining assessments (attendance note, advocacy and all written skills) will be marked by a solicitor. All assessors will have received training on how to assess a candidate's performance against the relevant criteria. It is therefore essential that you tackle your assessments in the same way that you would if you were a fully qualified solicitor on the first day of practice, ie with professionalism, confidence and calmness. This will come across to the assessors in the examination itself: remember that they are fundamentally assessing your suitability for practice!

WHERE DOES *REVISE SQE* COME INTO IT?

This new series of revision guides for SQE2 will provide you with helpful tips and advice on how to tackle each skill assessment in the relevant contexts. Each book provides a range of example threshold answers to SQE2-style assessment questions, which you can use to practise and assess your answers against, to see how you are performing in each individual area. This is designed to assist with your revision and consolidate your understanding of how key topics could be assessed in the SQE2 examinations. We hope that this series will give clarity for assessment focus, provide useful tips for sitting SQE2 and act as a general revision aid.

Finally, always keep in mind that while SQE2 is primarily a skills-based assessment, you are still being tested on your knowledge of the law. It is therefore important that you conduct an honest self-evaluation on the areas of the SQE1 specification with which you feel you need further support. *Revise SQE* can help you with this:

- Check out the 'SQE1 Revision Checklist' for each of our SQE1 revision guides on our website: **www.revise4law.co.uk**. These will help you to identify which substantive topics you feel confident about being assessed on, and which ones you need to revise.
- All of our *Revise SQE* revision guides are mapped to the relevant SRA specifications for SQE1. Before taking the SQE2 assessments, remember to look back at our revision guides for SQE1 if you have any gaps in your legal knowledge.

1

Case and matter analysis

MAKE SURE YOU KNOW

Case and matter analysis is a fundamental skill for any aspiring solicitor. It forms a core component of the SQE2 assessments, and you might be assessed on this skill in the context of criminal litigation on day one of the assessments (see the Introduction for more detail). Candidates are expected to demonstrate their ability to organise and evaluate relevant information to progress a case effectively. This includes understanding timelines, procedural requirements and decision-making. Managing a case efficiently is essential for client representation as well as for ensuring compliance with court directions and professional obligations. You will need to focus on case theory development, evidence reviews and procedural planning to approach this part of the SQE2 assessment.

All of your written legal skills assessments in criminal litigation will take place on day one of the assessment period. Before attempting the questions in this chapter, we recommend that you brush up your SQE1 FLK of criminal litigation by rereading ***Revise SQE: Criminal Law*** and ***Revise SQE: Criminal Practice***.

SQE ASSESSMENT ADVICE

As you work through this chapter, remember to pay particular attention in your revision to:

- identifying and analysing legally and factually relevant issues
- strategically organising information in a logical way that can be easily understood
- demonstrating a sound understanding of procedural rules
- ensuring your response is clear, accurate and concise
- tailoring your analysis to the client's objectives and the point of proceedings
- identifying any ethical or professional conduct issues that may arise.

See the Appendix for the SRA's performance indicators in case and matter analysis, and how to demonstrate your competency in this skill.

INTRODUCTION TO CASE AND MATTER ANALYSIS IN CRIMINAL LITIGATION

For the case and matter analysis assessment, you will be expected to produce a written report that gives a legal analysis of a case and provides client-focused advice. This part of SQE2 tests your ability to think critically and apply legal knowledge in a practical context. Your written analysis must be clear, concise and tailored to the intended audience. In the SQE2 case and matter analysis assessment, your analysis will be addressed to the partner of the firm and contain advice that they can quickly adopt to send to the client. As such, it must adopt language appropriate to both the partner and the client. You will have to demonstrate the ability to:

- extract key facts
- understand, condense and apply the relevant law, and
- present logical, well-structured reasoning.

Give yourself the best chance of success in your SQE2 case and matter analysis assessment by approaching the question in a structured manner. Try adopting the following method:

1. Identify the client's objectives and key issues raised in your instructions (the key issues will likely be in bold in your instructions, so pay close attention to them).
2. Use the materials provided and your legal knowledge to determine the relevant law and procedure.
3. Structure your analysis clearly, using headings and logical structure to guide the reader.
4. Tailor your advice to the client's needs, using plain English and appropriate tone. Lift the wording from your instructions to ensure that you are answering the client's queries.
5. Review your report for clarity, accuracy and professionalism, to meet the assessment criteria.

Assessment technique

Success in this assessment relies on presenting reasoning in a clear, logical and structured way. It is important to highlight relevant facts, legal issues and procedures in a way that is clear, concise and digestible for the reader. The clearer and more organised your analysis, the easier it is for the assessor to evaluate your understanding and how you apply the law in practice.

SQE2 case and matter analysis assessment criteria

Try to remember these points as you construct your answer, and refer back to them as you review our sample answers in this chapter:

Skills

1. Identify relevant facts.
2. Provide client-focused advice (ie advice which demonstrates an understanding of the problem from the client's point of view and what the client wants to achieve, not just from a legal perspective).
3. Use clear, precise, concise and acceptable language.

Application of law

4. Apply the law correctly to the client's situation.
5. Apply the law comprehensively to the client's situation.
6. Identify any ethical and professional conduct issues and exercise judgement to resolve them honestly and with integrity.

For further support and guidance on how to meet the SQE2 case and matter analysis assessment criteria, see ***Introduction to Written Legal Skills for SQE2***, chapter 1, Case and matter analysis.

In chapter 7 of ***Revise SQE: Criminal Law***, we considered the core principles of criminal liability in theft offences. Question 1 below demonstrates how your knowledge of this topic could be tested in the context and format of an SQE2 case and matter analysis assessment.

■ QUESTION 1

Email to candidate

From: Partner
Sent: 30 September 202#
To: Candidate
Subject: Theft by employee – Mr Daniel SMITH

You are instructed to represent Mr Daniel Smith, a 34-year-old warehouse operative charged with theft, contrary to s 1 of the Theft Act 1968.

The allegation
Mr Smith has worked at Voltora Distribution Ltd, a large electronic wholesaler, for over three years. He was arrested following an internal investigation triggered by inventory discrepancies: over a two-month period, the company reported missing stock valued at approximately £19,000, including smartphones, tablets and accessories.

The company reviewed CCTV footage and identified Mr Smith on multiple occasions removing boxes from the warehouse and placing them in his personal vehicle during his shifts. The footage does not show him scanning or logging the items through the company system, nor did he mention to any other staff member that he would be taking them personally to a customer.

The CCTV summary compiled by the security manager notes that, on two of the dates, Mr Smith appears to write on a small notepad before loading boxes. There are also two 'blind spots' where his movements are partly obstructed by shelving. On one occasion, he is seen looking at his phone while loading items, although it is unclear what he is doing. The footage has no audio.

Mr Smith was arrested at his home address, where the police seized:
- several unopened boxes of electronics that match the missing stock
- a company-issued scanner device
- a handwritten list of items and dates.

Mr Smith gave a no-comment interview at the police station on advice from his legal representative.

Our instructions
We are now instructed by Mr Smith privately. He denies theft and claims that he was acting under instruction from his former supervisor, Mr Cooper, who allegedly told him to move the stock to a temporary off-site location because of a system upgrade. Mr Smith says that he was never given written confirmation of this but that he trusted Mr Cooper as his supervisor. Mr Cooper has since resigned and moved abroad, and is currently uncontactable.

Mr Smith insists that he did not intend to permanently deprive the company of the items and believed that he was following legitimate instructions. He is very concerned about losing his job.

He also mentioned that other staff were aware of the stock movements, and that the company's inventory system often failed and had frequent errors.

One member of staff, Ms Jade Patel, provided a witness statement (Attachment 1). It has now been brought to our attention that Ms Patel has left the UK to work in Australia and will be unable to attend a trial. It has however been indicated that the statement could be admitted as hearsay.

The CPS has served initial disclosure, including:

- CCTV footage showing Mr Smith removing boxes on five separate occasions
- a statement from the warehouse manager confirming the missing stock and Mr Smith's access to the inventory system
- a forensic report that matches serial numbers of the recovered items to company records
- a CCTV report confirming recent maintenance due to previous faults in the system
- Ms Patel's witness statement with a notice of potential hearsay application.

Advice and analysis required
Mr Smith would like advice about his potential liability for theft, having regard to the strengths and weaknesses of the prosecution's case.

I would like you to provide advice and analysis to form the basis of a letter to the client. Mr Smith has no legal background and only a basic understanding of criminal proceedings. He would appreciate an explanation of the relevant law where you feel it is appropriate.

The advice should also focus on the legal and factual issues raised by the current disclosure. Please do not include detailed trial preparation, trial or sentencing advice at this stage. I have dealt with all client care matters, so you do not need to consider these.

Please set out your advice and analysis on the following:

1. **Based on the current disclosure, how strong is the prosecution case and what potential defences may be available to Mr Smith?**
2. **What further disclosure or reasonable lines of enquiry can we request of the prosecution?**
3. **What further evidence or information do we need from Mr Smith?**

Many thanks

Partner

Attachment:
Witness statement of Jade Patel

Attachment 1

STATEMENT OF WITNESS
(Criminal Procedure Rules, r 16.2; Criminal Justice Act 1967, s 9)

Name: Jade Patel
Age: Over 18

This statement, signed by me, is true to the best of my knowledge and belief and I make it knowing that if it is tendered in evidence I shall be liable to prosecution if I have wilfully stated in it anything which I know to be false or do not believe to be true.

I am Jade Patel. I was employed by Voltora Distribution Ltd as a warehouse operative for five years. I knew Daniel Smith ('Dan') as a colleague who worked similar shifts to me. We always got on well and had a good working relationship.

My duties included picking and packing electronic goods, scanning items through the inventory system and ensuring stock is logged correctly.

I recall an incident which took place in either late February or early March this year. I was working a late shift, which finished at 10 P.M. Dan was also on shift that day. I remember seeing him in the rear warehouse near the shuttered loading door. He had a pallet truck with several sealed boxes on it. I saw him move the boxes outside, towards the staff car park. It looked like he was loading the boxes into the boot of his grey car.

At the time, I did not question this. It was not unusual for staff to move stock to vans or storage areas when asked to do so. I just assumed that Dan had been asked to move them by a supervisor.

Our supervisor at the time, Mr Cooper, did sometimes give verbal instructions rather than putting things in writing. He often said that the inventory system was unreliable and that items would be scanned later or recorded manually if the system was down.

I couldn't say for certain what was in the boxes, and I did not inspect them. They were sealed and just looked like ordinary Voltora stock boxes.

I would like to add that the inventory system was sometimes faulty, failing to register items and shutting down unexpectedly. When this happened, Mr Cooper told us that he would 'sort it later'. We had previously raised concerns about inconsistent instructions from different supervisors and stock movements.

When the warehouse manager asked me in June whether I had seen anything unusual relating to stock, I told him what I remembered about Dan moving boxes to his car. I made it clear that I thought he was acting on instructions as I had no reason to suspect anything improper.

I have now left Voltora and am currently in Australia on a working visa. I do not know when I will be returning to the UK. I have been informed that I may be required to give evidence, but I cannot change my travel plans and am not in a position to attend court at present.

Signed: *Jade Patel*
Date: 30 August 202#

* * *

■ YOUR TURN

Have a go at answering question 1, remembering the guidance on page 1.

- Refer to the structured approach in the SRA's assessment criteria on page 2.
- Maintain a professional tone when writing, upholding the standard that would be expected of a solicitor advising a client and/or solicitor.
- Ensure that you apply the law accurately by clearly identifying and applying the relevant principles.
- Identify any ethical or professional conduct issues that might arise.
- Timings are important: you will need to prepare and write your answer in 60 minutes. Be mindful of how long you want to spend preparing, writing and reviewing your answer.

SQE1 Functioning legal knowledge link

Remember that the general principles of criminal law were considered in chapter 1 of ***Revise SQE: Criminal Law***, and chapter 7 focused specifically on the law of theft. Each element of the offence must first be proven before one can consider a defence. Consider whether the advice to the client should be that the prosecution cannot prove a certain element of the offence (eg dishonesty) or whether there is a separate defence excusing or justifying the client's liability.

EVALUATING YOUR ANSWER

When you have attempted question 1, mark it yourself against the SQE2 case and matter analysis assessment criteria. Do you think your attempt met the threshold standard?

Now compare your attempt with the following key legal points and two sample answers to the question. A circled number indicates that commentary is provided for this part of the answer. The commentary explains whether or not the sample answer satisfies the assessment criteria and is likely to meet the SQE2 threshold standard.

➥Key legal points: question 1

- Note that citations are generally not required but, as s 1 of the Theft Act 1968 is a listed authority in the SQE2 assessment specification, you may be expected to recite/recall that as part of your report to the partner. The offence of theft is made out where a person dishonestly appropriates property belonging to another with the intention of permanently depriving the other of it.
- The key question here is whether Mr Smith's actions amounted to theft contrary to s 1 of the Theft Act 1968 or whether he lacked the dishonest intent required for the offence owing to his belief that he was acting under instruction.

Evidential strengths and weaknesses of the case

- The main thing to assess in this scenario is dishonesty. The test for dishonesty is twofold:
  1. What was the defendant's actual belief as to the facts?
  2. Was the conduct dishonest by the standards of ordinary decent people?
- If Mr Smith genuinely believed that he was acting under instruction from his supervisor, dishonesty may be negated. However, the absence of any written instructions and the concealment of the items at Mr Smith's home may undermine his claim.
- The intention to permanently deprive can be inferred from the circumstances. If Mr Smith stored the items at home without informing the company or intending to return them, the prosecution case is strong.

- Based on the facts given, the prosecution will rely on the CCTV footage, recovery of items and lack of records, which are likely to establish appropriation and possession of property belonging to another. As the defence, you will have to focus on Mr Smith's belief and the context in which he acted.
- If you argue that Mr Smith was following instructions and had no dishonest intent, and this is believed, he may have a complete defence. At this point, you need to consider whether the belief was genuine and whether those actions were consistent with that belief.

Further evidence to be obtained

- Mr Smith's account relies on him acting under authority from his supervisor. You would need to seek evidence capable of supporting this, including messages, emails or calls with Mr Cooper.
- As the CPS may seek to rely on the witness statement of Ms Patel, you need evidence to challenge her availability to attend trial and the reliability of her account.
- You could explore weaknesses in continuity and CCTV reliability, such as blind spots and clarity of the footage, and seek access to any further maintenance logs that may be available.

SAMPLE ANSWER 1 TO QUESTION 1

Daniel Smith has been charged with theft contrary to s 1 of the Theft Act 1968. The allegation concerns the removal of high-value electronic goods from his employer, Voltora Distribution Ltd, at their warehouse over a two-month period. Mr Smith maintains that he was acting under the instructions of his former supervisor and did not intend to steal the items. This advice outlines the key legal and evidential issues, identifies further steps to support the defence and highlights any relevant ethical and professional matters for consideration. [1]

Legal and evidential issues [2]

To secure a conviction for theft, the prosecution must prove that Mr Smith:

1. Appropriated property,
2. Which belonged to another,
3. Dishonestly,
4. With the intention of permanently depriving the other of it. [3]

The first two elements are relatively straightforward on the current evidence. CCTV shows Mr Smith removing stock from the warehouse without logging it, and those items were subsequently found at his home address. These matters clearly establish appropriation and property belonging to another. Beyond these elements, there are strengths and weaknesses in the Crown's case that require careful analysis. [4]

Strengths in the Crown's case

- The prosecution can rely on the fact that Mr Smith removed items without completing the standard logging procedure. In an employment setting where there are procedures in place, such a breach may be argued to be inherently suspicious and inconsistent with acting under proper instruction. [5]
- The goods were found at Mr Smith's home rather than at another warehouse or company vehicle. This strongly supports the inference that items were not being moved as part of an official process.

- The lack of documentation, emails, messages or other communications confirming Mr Cooper's alleged instructions weakens Mr Smith's explanation. In a large company, stock movement for a 'system upgrade' would usually generate an audit trail and it is likely that the prosecution will rely upon this in Mr Cooper's absence. ❻

Potential defences available

- The CCTV report provided notes that there were blind spots due to shelving and that some of the cameras had undergone maintenance because of faults. This raises the questions of whether the footage gives a complete and reliable account of Mr Smith's movements and whether there are some parts missing from the CCTV recordings.
- Ms Patel's statement supports Mr Smith's case insofar as she states that she believed he was acting under instructions. If admitted, this is a favourable account to the defence. The CPS has indicated that it may seek to admit the statement as hearsay, which raises issues of admissibility, reliability and the weight that the court should place on such evidence. The key considerations for hearsay are whether reasonable steps have been taken to secure Ms Patel's attendance, whether her belief is based on direct knowledge or general practice and what weight should be given to her statement, considering she cannot be cross-examined.
- Mr Cooper, the alleged source of the instructions to move stock off site, has left the UK and has been unable to provide a statement. This is a substantial evidential gap in the prosecution case. There is no one else, on the facts thus far, who could contradict or corroborate Mr Smith's account. ❼

The test for dishonesty is twofold and requires both of the following to be made out:

1. What Mr Smith knew or believed at the time, and
2. Whether his conduct was dishonest by the standards of ordinary decent people. ❽

Mr Smith claims that he was instructed by his supervisor, Mr Cooper, to move the stock for a system upgrade. If this account is accepted, it may negate the dishonesty. However, the absence of written instructions, the concealment of the items and the resignation of Mr Cooper may weaken the defence.

The prosecution is also likely to submit that Mr Smith's actions demonstrate an intention to permanently deprive the company of the goods, particularly given the lack of communication with management and the storage of the items at his home. By contrast, the defence can emphasise that Mr Smith is likely to have been previously instructed by Mr Cooper in an informal manner such as verbally. Considering that the company was undergoing system changes, this may make Mr Smith's belief more credible. ❾

Further evidence required from prosecution and Mr Smith

To support Mr Smith's defence, I would recommend the following:

1. Request internal communications or logs that reference stock movement or any system changes that may have occurred.
2. Take a detailed proof of evidence from Mr Smith that explains his actions, beliefs and any efforts that he made to confirm the instructions from Mr Cooper. Clarify his understanding of company procedures and whether he received any training on inventory handling.
3. Attempt to ascertain more information about the company's working practices and Mr Cooper's management style, to discover whether it was the norm for employees to act on verbal instructions only.
4. Obtain further information relating to Ms Patel and her availability to attend trial. It would also be beneficial to collect evidence that could challenge the reliability of her account of what she saw, as the CPS may seek to rely on her witness statement.

All of this information will help to assess the credibility of Mr Smith's account and may support a defence based on lack of dishonest intent. ⑩

Conclusion

At this stage the prosecution case appears strong, but the defence could succeed if Mr Smith's belief in acting under his supervisor's instructions is accepted and properly evidenced. Further investigation into workplace practices, CCTV reliability, hearsay evidence and Mr Cooper's management style is essential to strengthen the position. Additional disclosure and witness evidence will be key to determining whether dishonesty and therefore theft can be proved. ⑪

COMMENTARY

① The opening paragraph clearly sets out the context and purpose of the advice. It includes the client's details, the charge against him and the structure of the report to follow. This is an excellent starting point for the analysis as it aligns with the SQE2 requirement for clarity and client-focused communication. The candidate has made the introduction clear for any reader.

② The use of headings throughout the answer demonstrates a logical approach and a professional structure. This helps the assessor to follow the legal reasoning and see where different aspects of the case details are covered.

③ The legal elements of theft are correctly identified, and listed in a way that avoids any complicated language. This shows a solid understanding of the legal principles here, as well as an ability to adapt to the audience so that a lay client can easily understand.

④ The application of the relevant law to the scenario is impressive and effectively done, noting that the first two elements of the offence are satisfied but that the Crown's case is not watertight with regard to the remaining elements. The reference to CCTV footage and possession of the goods is relevant, though the candidate could have deepened their analysis by discussing how this evidence will be used.

⑤ The writer makes good use of lists to show the balance between the strengths and weaknesses of the case. This is useful for the assessor to follow the advice and understand key issues that arise. This demonstrates logical thinking and highlights the relevant information effectively.

⑥ The candidate correctly applies facts to the law in the discussion around the absence of written instructions and concealment of items. This meets the criteria to weigh the strengths and weaknesses of the case.

⑦ Points 2 and 3 demonstrate a good working knowledge of legal principles relating to hearsay evidence and the admissibility of it. The candidate shows awareness of the importance of reliability and relevance of evidence, and the need to evaluate how evidence can be properly used in court.

⑧ The answer correctly identifies dishonesty as the central issue. This demonstrates an understanding of the principal law and how it operates in practice.

⑨ The identification of the prosecution case is good as it shows an understanding of analysis from both sides of the scenario. This touches on the relevant principles without going into too much detail or pre-empting the prosecution case before being fully aware of it.

⑩ The 'Further evidence' section is practical and identifies solid next steps that would support the defence case. The candidate demonstrates an understanding of how to strategically progress a case without being unrealistic in their prospects.

⑪ The conclusion summarises the position effectively and reinforces the need for further evidence and next steps to move the case forwards. It is concise and client-focused, and meets the requirements set out in the instructions.

Does this answer meet the threshold?

This sample answer would be likely to meet the SQE2 threshold standard. The language throughout is clear and professional whilst remaining accessible to the lay client, who the instructions state has little understanding of criminal proceedings. The tone is suitable for the solicitor who will receive the email, and they will easily be able to use this information and advice to form the basis of a letter to the client.

The candidate accurately identifies the legal principles and applies them to the facts sufficiently. The analysis is thorough, well-reasoned and logically structured, providing a comprehensive evaluation that meets the requirements of the SQE2 assessment. The response shows sound professional judgement and would be considered competent at the expected standard.

Now consider the second sample answer to question 1.

■ SAMPLE ANSWER 2 TO QUESTION 1

Mr Smith has been charged with theft from his employer, Voltora Distribution Ltd. He says that he did not steal anything and that he was just doing what his supervisor, Mr Cooper, told him to do. Apparently, he was moving stock around because of a system upgrade which meant that stock needed to be moved. Some of the missing items were found at his house and as such he is now being prosecuted for theft. ❶

The law

In law, theft is when someone takes something that doesn't belong to them and doesn't give it back. ❷ If Mr Smith can prove that he didn't mean to steal, then he might not be guilty. ❸ The court must decide in this case if he was being dishonest in his actions or not. If he thought that he was doing what he was told, then it is possible that he was not being dishonest.

Evidence

The defence needs to obtain evidence capable of supporting Mr Smith's claim that he acted under instruction, including statements from colleagues, internal communications or records of system upgrades. It is important to gather and review the evidence to gain a clearer picture of the prosecution case. ❹

Next steps

We should try to find out if anyone knew about this. Perhaps Mr Cooper told other people the same thing and he can be found at fault. ❺ If there are emails or messages that could help then we need them. Mr Smith should also be asked to write down everything that he remembers about what Mr Cooper said to him and when he said it. ❻

Conclusion

Mr Smith contends that he did nothing wrong and that he was following instructions from his supervisor. We need to be able to build a case that signals this fact so that he is not found guilty of theft. It doesn't look good though that items were found at his house. ❼ We need more information on this case before we can proceed any further. ❽

COMMENTARY

1. The opening paragraph provides a basic summary of the facts but it lacks professional tone and structure. It reads more like a casual narrative than a formal legal document, and this tone continues throughout the answer. There is no clear statement of the purpose of the advice or identification of the legal issues that are to be addressed.
2. The explanation of theft does not cite the legislation correctly under the Theft Act 1968. The explanation is also too simplistic and does not actually set out the elements of the offence. Some of the phrasing is vague and could be construed as misleading. This does not demonstrate a sound understanding of the legal principles and would likely fail to meet the competency standard for legal application to the facts.
3. In stating 'If Mr Smith can prove . . .' there is a misrepresentation as to the criminal burden of proof. The burden is on the prosecution to prove guilty so that a jury is sure (historically known as 'beyond reasonable doubt'). The defendant does not have to prove his innocence. This is a fundamental error in the understanding of criminal procedure and would probably be marked down significantly.
4. This paragraph demonstrates a practical approach to gathering evidence, showing an understanding of the type of material that could support the defence position and challenge the prosecution case. However, the answer makes no reference to the witness statement of Ms Patel. This is disappointing, as it is a key piece of evidence that the candidate would be required to consider in order to provide a complete and balanced assessment of the case.
5. The suggestion that the solicitors should find out if anyone else was aware of the activities is correct, but this could be more detailed and developed further. It could identify the specific evidence which is required to develop the defence. The candidate could have mentioned further evidence, such as how to secure details of the internal procedures and training records, and challenges to the prosecution evidence that would support the defence case.
6. The candidate is correct to ask Mr Smith to write down his recollection of recent events, but this could be developed further, giving specifics of what is required from Mr Smith so that his account would be concise and only include relevant information. The candidate could also explain how this evidence would be used to advance the case.
7. Saying that 'it doesn't look good' is not appropriate language, and instead the candidate should identify and/or manage the implications of this kind of statement. This part of the answer would have been strengthened if the candidate had mentioned the ethical issues raised, as required by the assessment criteria: the solicitor's duty to act both independently and in the client's best interests.
8. The conclusion is vague and unprofessional. It should summarise the legal position and give advice on next steps clearly, to assist in progressing the case forwards. On the whole this answer is far too short to satisfy the assessment criteria and does not appropriately advise on the matters at hand.

Does this answer meet the threshold?

This answer lacks the structure, legal accuracy, analytical depth and professional tone required to meet the SQE2 case and matter analysis standard. It demonstrates insufficient legal knowledge, poor application of law to facts and weak ethical awareness. To pass, the candidate would need to significantly improve the legal reasoning, structure and clarity of advice.

Below is another example of a different scenario and possible question that you may be asked for the SQE2 case and matter analysis assessment.

■ QUESTION 2

Email to candidate

From: Partner
Sent: 06 July 202#
To: Candidate
Subject: Ms Donna WESTBURY

We act for Ms Donna Westbury, a 43-year-old woman charged with criminal damage, contrary to s 1 of the Criminal Damage Act 1971. The charge relates to an incident that occurred two months ago at a local council office in Nottingham. Ms Westbury allegedly smashed a glass panel in the reception area of the council building, using a chair that she took from behind the desk. The value of the damage is approximately £1,200.

The incident was witnessed by two council employees and was captured on CCTV. Ms Westbury was arrested at the scene and taken to the police station, where she gave a no-comment interview after seeking legal advice. Ms Westbury was later charged and initially granted bail. The CPS has now served the CCTV footage, witness statements and a repair invoice from the council. The first hearing, where a plea will be expected, has been listed for two weeks' time.

We have met Ms Westbury on several occasions, and she can be temperamental in nature. She has a long-standing diagnosis of paranoid schizophrenia and has previously been detained under the Mental Health Act 1983. Ms Westbury was discharged from a psychiatric unit six weeks before the incident and we are told that she has not been engaging with the programme set by her community mental health services. She is currently not taking her prescribed medication and tells us that she cannot remember the last time she took it – she claims that it makes her feel 'spaced out' when she does take it.

It has been noted that, during meetings with us, Ms Westbury has displayed disorganised thinking, paranoia and delusional beliefs. She claims that the council is part of a larger conspiracy to monitor her behaviour, and she insists that the damage was a necessary act of protest for her own safety. It has been difficult to communicate with Ms Westbury as she frequently becomes agitated and refuses to discuss the evidence. She is yet to review the CCTV footage.

Although Ms Westbury is currently on bail, we have concerns about whether she is likely to continue complying with her bail conditions in light of her mental health presentation, disengagement with treatment and agitation. We are concerned that her behaviour may lead the prosecution to make an application to vary or revoke her bail. This could lead to her being remanded in custody at the first hearing.

At present, we have been unable to obtain coherent instructions from Ms Westbury and as a result cannot prepare the case effectively. We are also aware that her mental state may be deteriorating, particularly as she has not been engaging with her mental health treatment.

I would like you to prepare a written analysis that addresses the following points:

1. **Whether I am right to be concerned about Ms Westbury's current bail status and the risk of her bail being revoked or varied at her first hearing, particularly given her presentation and lack of engagement.**
2. **The legal framework governing bail, including the factors that the court considers when deciding whether to grant bail, impose conditions or remand in custody.**
3. **The best course of action regarding communication with Ms Westbury. Do any conduct or ethical issues arise from this?**

Before you write your analysis and advice, please read carefully the custody record document (Attachment 1) and the witness statement by a community mental health nurse (Attachment 2), and evaluate whether these documents might help to determine whether bail may be varied or revoked in criminal proceedings.

Please ensure that your analysis is clear, concise and well structured. You are encouraged to refer to relevant legal principles, procedural rules and any other obligations that are appropriate.

Many thanks

Partner

Attachments:

1. Custody record of Donna Westbury
2. Witness statement of Janet Batty, community mental health nurse

Attachment 1

Custody record of Donna Westbury

Name: Donna Westbury
DOB: 03/04/1983
Police station: Nottingham Central Police Station
Date of arrest: 05/05/202#
Offence: Criminal Damage – s 1 Criminal Damage Act 1971

Risk assessment
Mental health flag: Yes – paranoid schizophrenia
Substance misuse: None reported
Suicide/self-harm risk: Low. No current intent but history of self-harm is noted
Violence risk: Moderate. Recent agitation and property damage noted

Custodial behaviour
Ms Westbury arrived in custody agitated and speaking in a paranoid manner. She claimed that the police and council were 'part of a conspiracy against her'. She refused to sit in the interview room initially, but later calmed down and entered after reassurance. There was no aggressive physical contact, but verbal threats directed towards inanimate objects were noted. Complied with basic instructions but presented as distracted.

Medication
Ms Westbury is prescribed anti-psychotic medication but she is not currently taking this. She has been offered a medical review but declined.

Bail considerations
Initial bail granted: Yes – with conditions to reside at address, report to police and not to contact the council. Risk of non-compliance due to mental health deterioration, non-engagement and agitation.

Additional comments
Ms Westbury is capable of understanding bail conditions, but compliance is unclear. There are no immediate concerns for harm to self or others in custody.

Signed: *PC Omari Thompson*
Date: 6 May 202#

Attachment 2

STATEMENT OF WITNESS

(Criminal Procedure Rules, r 16.2; Criminal Justice Act 1967, s 9)

Name: Janet Batty
Age: Over 18

This statement, signed by me, is true to the best of my knowledge and belief and I make it knowing that if it is tendered in evidence I shall be liable to prosecution if I have wilfully stated in it anything which I know to be false or do not believe to be true.

I am Janet Batty, employed as a community mental health nurse. I have been involved in the care and treatment of Ms Donna Westbury since her discharge from the mental health unit on 20 March 202#. I am providing this statement in connection with the ongoing criminal proceedings against Ms Westbury for alleged criminal damage.

History
Ms Westbury is a 43-year-old woman with a long-standing diagnosis of paranoid schizophrenia. She has previously been detained under the Mental Health Act 1983 and has a history of admissions for acute episodes of psychosis.

Engagement with services
Ms Westbury was allocated a care plan when she was discharged from inpatient care and she was expected to engage with our team for ongoing treatment. Since discharge, she has not engaged consistently with our service and reports that she has not been taking her prescribed medication, stating that it makes her feel 'spaced out'. She is unable to recall when she last took her medication.

Current prescription
During our meetings, Ms Westbury has displayed the following:

- disorganised thinking and difficulty in maintaining communication
- paranoid beliefs and justification for her actions
- agitation, including refusal to discuss her medication and the alleged incident.

Risk assessment
Given her current mental state, lack of engagement and ongoing paranoia, there is a concern relating to Ms Westbury's ability to comply with bail conditions. I am concerned about her mental health deteriorating further and thus impacting her judgement and decision-making. Close monitoring and support are required to manage her condition and reduce the risk of breaching bail conditions.

My observations are intended to assist any considerations relating to bail status, risk management and ongoing mental health care needs.

Signed: *Janet Batty*
Date: 30 June 202#

* * *

■ YOUR TURN

Have a go at answering question 2, remembering the guidance on page 1.

- Refer to the structured approach in the SRA's assessment criteria on page 2.
- Maintain a professional tone when writing, upholding the standard that would be expected of a solicitor advising a client and/or solicitor.
- Ensure that you apply the law accurately by clearly identifying and applying the relevant principles.
- Identify any ethical or professional conduct issues that might arise.
- Timings are important: you will need to prepare and write your answer in 60 minutes. Be mindful of how long you want to spend preparing, writing and reviewing your answer.

SQE1 Functioning legal knowledge link

The general principles of criminal damage were considered in chapter 9 of ***Revise SQE: Criminal Law***, and chapter 2 of ***Revise SQE: Criminal Practice*** focuses specifically on bail applications. Refer to these books to refresh your functioning legal knowledge of the principles in this question. The elements of criminal damage must be identifiable in order to present a clear case analysis as required and answer the question to a sufficient level of competence. You should also consider the presumption in favour of bail and whether it is applicable in this question.

EVALUATING YOUR ANSWER

When you have attempted question 2, mark it yourself against the SQE2 case and matter analysis assessment criteria. Do you think your attempt met the threshold standard?

Now compare your attempt with the following key legal points and two sample answers to the question. A circled number indicates that commentary is provided for this part of the answer. The commentary explains whether or not the sample answer satisfies the assessment criteria and is likely to meet the SQE2 threshold standard.

➥Key legal points: question 2

- The central issue in this scenario is whether Ms Westbury's bail status might be challenged. This is an increasingly common issue that junior practitioners now have to navigate, and, whilst in some cases junior solicitors will have the assistance of counsel, in many 'low-level' cases heard in the magistrates' court they will be on their own.
- The right to bail is governed primarily by the Bail Act 1976 and relevant provisions in the Criminal Procedure Rules. Bail may be granted unless there is just cause to refuse it. When considering the exceptions to bail, the court must consider only those exceptions that are relevant to the offence in question. Low-value criminal damage is a summary imprisonable offence; therefore, only the exceptions under that heading may be included, which are:
  - The defendant has been previously granted bail and has failed to surrender, and the court believes that the defendant would fail to surrender to custody.
  - The defendant was on bail at the time of the offence and there are substantial grounds for believing that they would commit an offence whilst on bail.
  - The court is satisfied that being remanded in custody would be for the defendant's own protection.

- The court must consider the character, antecedents, associations and ties of the defendant in respect of compliance with bail. This can include non-engagement with treatment or medication, agitation or unpredictable behaviour and vulnerability.
- Conditions can only be imposed if they are necessary to mitigate the concerns of the court (s 3(6) Bail Act). Conditions could include reporting requirements, resident restrictions, prohibition on contact with certain people and compliance with medical programmes.
- Bail decisions are made by the magistrates or district judge, who may consider both prosecution and defence submissions. The court may adjourn or vary bail conditions if any new risks emerge.
- It is the role of a solicitor to advise their client of the obligations under bail and consequences of non-compliance. They should consider applying to vary conditions in support of compliance. Ultimately, the solicitor should act in the client's best interests.
- The solicitor must consider what adjustments they should make when communicating with the client to respect their mental health difficulties. Furthermore, the solicitor must balance the need to maintain the confidentiality of the client whilst also not misleading the court.

■ SAMPLE ANSWER 1 TO QUESTION 2

I have been asked to advise on the position of our client, Ms Donna Westbury, following her charge of criminal damage contrary to s 1 of the Criminal Damage Act 1971, and whether she may face a challenge to her bail status ahead of the first hearing in two weeks' time. The charge arises from an incident at a local council office, where Ms Westbury allegedly caused damage to council property valued at approximately £1,200. Ms Westbury has a long-standing diagnosis of paranoid schizophrenia and has recently stopped taking her prescribed mental health treatments. Her behaviour during meetings has raised concerns about her ability to comply with bail conditions and to engage constructively with the proceedings.

This analysis will consider the issues relating to bail compliance, risk factors and appropriate steps that should be taken by her legal representative. ❶

Legal framework ❷

Bail is governed primarily by the Bail Act 1976. Where a person is charged with a criminal offence, there is a presumption in favour of bail, which applies up until the point that they either plead guilty or are found guilty. There are a number of exceptions to the presumption in favour of bail and, as criminal damage is an either-way offence, the exceptions under indictable offences would normally apply. However, £1,200 amounts to 'low-value' criminal damage and therefore only exceptions under summary imprisonable offences would apply. This might be more favourable to Ms Westbury's situation. The court may refuse or revoke bail where:

- The defendant has been previously granted bail and failed to surrender, and the court believes that they would fail to surrender again.
- The defendant was on bail at the time of the offence and there are substantial grounds for believing that they would commit an offence whilst on bail.
- The court is satisfied that being remanded in custody would be for the defendant's own protection. ❸

The court may grant bail unconditionally, grant bail with conditions or refuse bail altogether. The court has a broad power as to what kind of conditions it can impose. Where there is concern about a defendant's mental health, the court may impose specific conditions to mitigate risk, such as residing at a specified address, reporting to police stations and avoiding contact with particular individuals or places. However, mental health issues can also increase risk factors such as reoffending or non-compliance with conditions. A judge could consider evidence, reports and custody records when determining whether bail arrangements require modification. ❹

Risk assessment

Based upon the information provided, several factors indicate a heightened risk regarding bail compliance. Ms Westbury has stopped taking prescribed medication and has not engaged with her community mental health team. She has exhibited agitation, disorganisation and delusional beliefs, which may impair her understanding of or adherence to bail conditions.

While there is no evidence of prior bail breaches, her recent behaviour as described in her custody record and the witness statement of the community mental health nurse, Ms Batty, indicates a potential risk that may need further investigation. My concern would be that if something triggers a mental health breakdown Ms Westbury may become more unpredictable and more of a risk to the public. It is important for both Ms Westbury and her case that she is able to engage fully in proceedings, and as her legal representatives we should do all that we can to ensure this. ❺

Bail at the first hearing

Where an individual has been charged and bailed by the police, the court will generally continue with bail unless there is new information that challenges the status quo. The court could vary the bail conditions by imposing residence monitoring, reporting or other conditions. If the court is concerned that Ms Westbury may harm herself as a result of her mental health difficulties, it might apply the exception noted above and keep her in custody for her own protection. ❻

Should the prosecution object to bail, given the custody record and the statement of the community mental health nurse, we will need to put forward a number of counter arguments to act in the best interests of Ms Westbury. It would be my advice to highlight the mitigating factors such as Ms Westbury's lack of prior criminal history, cooperation with legal advice and willingness to comply with reasonable conditions. It may be useful to apply for specific mental health-related conditions which would facilitate compliance, such as mental health services supervision. ❼

On the facts thus far, it is unclear whether Ms Westbury has strong ties to the community or whether there are dependants or others involved, which would reduce the risk of her absconding. Furthermore, it would be helpful to find out more about Ms Westbury's background, which could be used as mitigation when it comes to an application for bail. ❽

Communication and ethical considerations

Given Ms Westbury's mental health condition, communication must be handled with care, with our advice set out clearly and in a non-confrontational manner. We should consider involving a mental health advocate to support her during meetings, to ensure that she is able to cooperate and understand sufficiently.

Under the SRA Code of Conduct, we have a duty to act in the best interests of the client and to uphold the proper administration of justice. If we are unable to obtain coherent instructions, we must consider whether we can continue to act on this matter. We may need to inform the court of these concerns while maintaining client confidentiality and acting in her best interest as far as possible. Importantly, we must not mislead the court regarding any concerns about Ms Westbury's behaviour. (9)

Conclusion

In my view, there is a strong basis for Ms Westbury to continue with bail despite the concerns, if it can be identified that she would comply with stringent conditions.

In the meantime, I recommend adapting communication to Ms Westbury's needs and consulting a specialist to advise on the best way to approach the case.

I also recommend obtaining a medical report that evidences Ms Westbury's mental health conditions and likelihood of compliance, and communicating it to the court and CPS at the earliest opportunity to ensure that she is dealt with proportionately. (10)

COMMENTARY

(1) The introduction clearly identifies the client, the charge and the purpose of the analysis that the candidate is writing. It sets out the factual background concisely and it appropriately explores the legal issue in the case, demonstrating a generally competent understanding of the legal and procedural issues surrounding bail in criminal proceedings. This meets the assessment criteria requirement for clarity and relevance, and provides an excellent opening for the assessor.

(2) The sample answer is well structured and makes good use of headings to address the areas requested by the partner.

(3) The candidate correctly identifies the legal framework under the Bail Act 1976. The list of criteria is accurate and well presented in a digestible manner. The candidate is aware of the specific rule that applies to low-value criminal damage and expresses it accurately.

(4) The application to Ms Westbury's circumstances demonstrates an understanding of how the test should be applied in practice. The analysis could be improved by more explicitly linking each element of the test to the client's behaviour, but this omission would not be detrimental to the candidate's outcome.

(5) This section is accurate and well argued. The candidate demonstrates a good understanding of the procedure and explains it in a clear and appropriate manner. The candidate could have strengthened their response by giving more detail of the conditions that would be the most likely or suitable to be assessed for and imposed on Ms Westbury.

(6) The candidate demonstrates a strong knowledge of the law in this area, citing one of the exceptions that may be applied specifically to Ms Westbury's case.

(7) The candidate uses the documents provided as part of the assessment paper - the custody record and the witness statement from the community mental health nurse - to support their advice and highlight the potential concerns that the court may raise with granting bail.

(8) This section clearly indicates the further information that would be helpful for the defence case in relation to mitigation. This is a proactive request and deals with some of the key bail considerations well. The candidate's response could be further developed by explaining the other considerations in more detail, but it does identify the most relevant points. However, note that in the Conclusion at the end of this answer the candidate does not include their suggestion to find out more about the defendant's background. When reviewing your answer, make sure that your conclusion includes all points of advice you have suggested.

9 The candidate successfully demonstrates their understanding of the relevant principles in the SRA Code of Conduct and the solicitor's duty. The suggestion to involve a mental health advocate is an appropriate point of professional conduct and shows a sensitivity to the client and her needs. This is well written and easy to follow.

10 The conclusion is practical and forward-looking. It summarises the key recommendations and next steps for the assessor, and provides a clear and precise conclusion of the candidate's client-focused advice. This meets the assessment criteria and reflects a good level of judgement and legal understanding.

Does this answer meet the threshold?

This answer would be likely to meet the passing threshold for the case and matter analysis assessment. It is legally sound and well structured, demonstrating an excellent application of legal principles to the facts given. The candidate makes good use of the information given and structures their response with subheadings to ensure clarity for the reader. Each section addresses a specific part of the task and the conclusion effectively summarises most of the recommendations.

Now consider the second sample answer to question 2.

■ SAMPLE ANSWER 2 TO QUESTION 2

I have reviewed the matter concerning Ms Donna Westbury, who is charged with criminal damage under s 1 of the Criminal Damage Act 1971. The incident involves damage to council property and the first hearing is scheduled to take place in two weeks' time. 1

Ms Westbury has a history of mental health issues including paranoid schizophrenia and has not been taking her medication. She has shown signs of paranoia and confusion during meetings and has been unable to give clear instructions. This raised concerns about her bail status and whether it could be varied or revoked.

Bail applications

Bail is governed primarily by the Bail Act 1976. The court may refuse or revoke bail where there is a substantial risk that the defendant may:

- fail to surrender to custody
- commit further offences
- interfere with witnesses or obstruct justice
- pose a risk to the safety of the public. 2

Procedure and outcomes

The court is likely to consider custody records, witness statements, her mental health history and engagement with treatment when deciding if bail should continue, be varied or be revoked. In cases where risk is seen as unmanageable, the defendant would be remanded to custody until a further bail application is made or until the completion of a trial and any sentencing that may arise. 3

At the first hearing, the defence should emphasise the defendant's willingness to comply with all that is being asked of her, as well as her lack of previous criminal history and the potential benefits of imposing supportive conditions rather than remand. 4

There is a risk to bail compliance but this can be managed with appropriate conditions, careful communication and liaison with the court and CPS. The defence should be prepared to respond to the prosecution application and ensure that the court is fully aware of all circumstances of the defendant's mental health and lifestyle, including likeliness to comply. ❺

Communicating with the client

There are concerns about Ms Westbury's engagement with legal advice. I think we need to ensure that we give her plenty of time to discuss matters as opposed to rushing through things. Importantly, we owe a duty to Ms Westbury and we should not inform the court of any of our own concerns regarding the risk of her non-compliance. ❻

Conclusion

I am of the view that Ms Westbury is capable of maintaining the same bail conditions. However, the court might think that more stringent bail conditions would be suitable to ensure that Ms Westbury is maintaining a stable mental state. This could be an appropriate middle ground where the risk is reduced whilst allowing her to remain at liberty. ❼

COMMENTARY

❶ The introduction begins well - it identifies the client and the charge - but it lacks detail and precision. This section could have included relevant facts such as the nature of the damage for clarity and accuracy from the outset.

❷ The candidate correctly identifies that bail is the central issue in the scenario but fails to recognise that the 'common' objections to bail (eg substantial grounds for believing the defendant will commit further offences) do not apply to low-level criminal damage. This is an immediate indication that they do not have a strong understanding of the functioning legal knowledge, which will result in them providing legally inaccurate advice. Furthermore, there is no discussion of how bail may be imposed, conditionally or otherwise, or how non-compliance might increase risk factors.

❸ The candidate refers to the custody record and witness statement but only does so generally. They do not specifically refer to or use the documents provided as part of the assessment paper.

❹ The explanation of procedure is too simplistic here. This lacks the clarity and depth that would be expected in this type of written document. To demonstrate their competency, the candidate should include how the court weighs risk factors against liberty, and how the defence can proactively advocate for supportive bail conditions to reduce risk without resorting to remand.

❺ This section could be more analytical and demonstrate a fuller understanding of the implications of revoking or varying bail. The candidate shows a clear understanding of risk mitigation, but this analysis could be developed further to link the client's behaviour to specific risks.

❻ The candidate discusses to some extent the communication needs and ethical issues that arise in the assessment. However, the discussion is vague and does not provide sufficient engagement with the issue at hand. From an ethical viewpoint, the candidate does not strike the right balance between maintaining client confidentiality and not misleading the court.

❼ The conclusion is rather confusing in that it contradicts itself. The first sentence mentions maintaining the same conditions whilst the second states that there could be more added. More clarity is important here so that the assessor knows what is being advised.

Does this answer meet the threshold?

This answer would not meet the SQE2 threshold standard. While it demonstrates a basic awareness of the issues, it lacks the depth, precision and professionalism required for competent legal practice. The legal framework is oversimplified and legally inaccurate, and the application to the client's specific circumstances is vague and underdeveloped. In places the tone is informal and, while suitable headings have been used to bring clarity, the report does not reflect the analysis required at this level. To achieve the SQE2 threshold, the candidate should demonstrate a more detailed understanding of the law and apply it clearly and logically to the facts.

■ KEY POINT CHECKLIST

This chapter has covered the following key knowledge points:

- The SQE2 assessment criteria for case and matter analysis and how to apply them in the context of criminal litigation.
- A suggested structure for approaching an SQE2 case and matter analysis question in criminal litigation.
- Examples of case and matter analysis responses that are either likely or unlikely to meet the threshold standard, with full commentary on their strengths and weaknesses.

■ SUMMARY AND REFLECTION

This chapter emphasises the importance of understanding the client's objectives, identifying legal and procedural issues and exercising judgement. A key takeaway is the importance of applying these principles to realistic fact patterns. You will need to demonstrate legal knowledge as well as your ability to prioritise issues, calculate how risks might be managed and propose practical next steps.

Success in this SQE2 written assessment requires more than legal accuracy - it demands clarity, structure and a client-centred approach. Practising with different scenarios is essential to developing the analytical and communication skills expected of a Day One Solicitor. As with all legal writing, a solid, logical structure will help you to achieve clarity and precision in your work, and allow you to show the assessor how you have arrived at your conclusions.

2

Legal research

■ MAKE SURE YOU KNOW

This chapter covers the skill of legal research in the context of criminal litigation, on which you may be assessed during day one of the SQE2 assessments. By its very nature, the SQE2 legal research assessment may require you to grapple with areas of law not specifically covered by the SQE1 specification. It is therefore important that you have a firm grasp of the basic principles of criminal law - actus reus, mens rea, causation and general defences - as these are universally applicable to a great number of criminal offences that you may be faced with in the assessment.

You may find it useful to refer to chapters 1–4 of ***Revise SQE: Criminal Law*** and chapters 1 and 3 of ***Revise SQE: Criminal Practice*** before attempting the questions in this chapter. Equipping yourself with a sound understanding of the foundations of criminal law and practice will allow you to commence the legal research task from the strongest position.

■ SQE ASSESSMENT ADVICE

As you work through this chapter, remember to pay particular attention to:

- including relevant facts in your answers
- identifying and using credible and relevant sources which support your advice
- tailoring your advice to the client's needs based upon their specific issue
- writing in a clear and concise manner, maintaining professionalism throughout
- providing a comprehensive analysis of the key issues that the client may face
- the way in which ethical or professional conduct issues are identified and resolved.

See the Appendix for the SRA's performance indicators in legal research and how to demonstrate your competency in this skill.

■ INTRODUCTION TO LEGAL RESEARCH IN CRIMINAL LITIGATION

On the day of the assessment, you will be asked to investigate a legal problem for a client. The question will take the form of an email from a partner requesting you to research an issue and provide the results of that research. Your aim in answering the assessment task is to write a note to the partner that explains your legal reasoning, the key sources you relied on and the advice you believe the partner should give to the client.

While the topic will fall under the broad heading of criminal litigation, it may require research beyond what you already know, so you will need to explore the additional resources provided in the assessment materials. Those resources will include both primary sources (such as statute and case law) and secondary sources (such as articles or commentaries). Some of these sources may not be directly relevant to the issue at hand, so you will need to determine which ones are most helpful.

You will have 60 minutes to complete the task, and there is no need to provide a detailed research trail. Your focus should be on delivering a clear, well-reasoned explanation and offering practical advice based on your research.

To succeed in your SQE2 legal research assessment, we recommend approaching the question in a structured manner. Try adopting the following method:

1. Identify the central theme of the issue: what questions need to be answered? Note this down.
2. Identify the relevant sources. Find the extracts from the sources that are relevant and decide how they will be referenced and incorporated into your answer.
3. Outline the law applicable to the questions raised by the central issue.
4. Apply that law to the facts of the problem: what does this mean for the client?
5. Identify the key steps applied in the relevant sources and write your answer to the question, ensuring that it relates back to and answers the questions you identified in point 1 above.
6. Conclude by suggesting to the partner a course of action appropriate to your views.
7. Review your answer, keeping in mind the question and the SQE2 legal research assessment criteria.

Assessment technique

Structure your research note clearly and guide the assessor through your reasoning: presenting a logical response demonstrates your ability to analyse the law and communicate your findings effectively. Remember to reference the sources provided and show how they support the conclusions that you have drawn.

SQE2 legal research assessment criteria

Try to remember these points as you construct your answer, and refer back to them as you review our sample answers in this chapter:

Skills

1. Identify and use relevant sources and information.
2. Provide advice which is client-focused and addresses the client's problem.
3. Use clear, precise, concise and acceptable language.

Application of law

4. Apply the law correctly to the client's situation.
5. Apply the law comprehensively to the client's situation.
6. Identify any ethical and professional conduct issues and exercise judgement to resolve them honestly and with integrity.

For further support and guidance on how to meet the SQE2 legal research assessment criteria, see ***Introduction to Written Legal Skills for SQE2***, chapter 2, Legal research.

Question 1 focuses on the offence of causing unnecessary suffering to a protected animal contrary to s 4(1) Animal Welfare Act 2006. You will see that both sample answers use the same logic to arrive at the correct answer but the key difference is the *demonstration* of the candidate's legal research, which is required to meet the SQE2 assessment criteria.

The sample questions in this chapter include six sources each for you to consider but bear in mind that the SQE2 assessment might include up to eight sources.

■ QUESTION 1

Email to candidate

From: Partner
Sent: 9 February 202#
To: Candidate
Subject: James Smith - New client enquiry

A new client, James, telephoned me this morning. He has been postally requisitioned for two offences of causing unnecessary suffering to animals contrary to s 4(1) Animal Welfare Act 2006.

He explained to me that his dogs, Alpha and Bravo, got into a fight in his back garden. He is not sure how the fight started but he heard it from inside the house and saw it from an upstairs window. In an apparent effort to scare the dogs, he picked up his air rifle to fire a warning shot. Not thinking his rifle was loaded, he pointed the gun at Alpha and pulled the trigger. The rifle was loaded; Alpha was shot in the head and appeared to die instantly.

James ran downstairs and out into the garden. Bravo was still attacking Alpha's now-dead body. James kicked him to the head and Bravo collapsed on top of Alpha. James kicked him again to move him. James could hear Bravo whimpering.

James took both dogs to the vets. Alpha was confirmed to be dead, and the vet noted he would have died instantly. Bravo was found to have a fractured skull and a bleed on the brain. The vet made a report to the RSPCA.

James has been charged with two offences of causing unnecessary suffering: one charge in respect of Alpha and one in respect of Bravo. Bravo remains in intensive care at a veterinary hospital, his care being funded by a 'crowdfunder page' set up by James.

James would like to know whether he has committed the offences with which he is charged.

Based on the information above and the sources provided, please research the answer to this question. Please report back to me so that I can advise the client.

You should include, for my reference, your legal reasoning, mentioning any key sources or authorities.

Many thanks,

Partner

Note to candidates:

You do not need to address any other offences that may or may not arise on the facts.

Given the time constraints of this assessment, we have not provided the full text of some primary sources. For the purposes of this assessment, where the full text of a

primary source is not provided, candidates may nevertheless cite the primary source on the basis it is referred to in one or more of the secondary sources provided and the full text can be checked at a later date.

Information displayed is as obtained on the date of search, for example purposes only. Information herein is not to be relied upon outside the purposes of this sample question.

Attachments

You have been provided with the following sources listed alphabetically in order of source name. The order of presentation is not intended as a guide to the order in which they should be consulted.

PLEASE NOTE THAT PART OR ALL OF SOME OF THESE SOURCES MAY NOT BE RELEVANT TO ANSWERING THE QUESTION

1. Animal Welfare Act 2006, ss 1–4, 62
2. *Bandeira and Brannigan v RSPCA* [2000] CO 2066/99
3. *DM* [2023] EWCA Crim 150
4. *Gray v RSPCA* [2013] EWHC 500 (Admin)
5. *Halsbury's Laws of England*, Animals, vol. 2, paras 144, 146
6. *Isted v Crown Prosecution Service* [1998] 162 JP 513

* * *

Source 1

Animal Welfare Act 2006, ss 1–4, 62

1 Animals to which the Act applies

(1) In this Act, except subsections (4) and (5), 'animal' means a vertebrate other than man.
(2) Nothing in this Act applies to an animal while it is in its foetal or embryonic form.
(3) The appropriate national authority may by regulations for all or any of the purposes of this Act—
  (a) extend the definition of 'animal' so as to include invertebrates of any description;
  (b) make provision in lieu of subsection (2) as respects any invertebrates included in the definition of 'animal';
  (c) amend subsection (2) to extend the application of this Act to an animal from such earlier stage of its development as may be specified in the regulations.
(4) The power under subsection (3)(a) or (c) may only be exercised if the appropriate national authority is satisfied, on the basis of scientific evidence, that animals of the kind concerned are capable of experiencing pain or suffering.
(5) In this section, 'vertebrate' means any animal of the Sub-phylum Vertebrata of the Phylum Chordata and 'invertebrate' means any animal not of that Sub-phylum.

2 'Protected animal'

An animal is a 'protected animal' for the purposes of this Act if—
(a) it is of a kind which is commonly domesticated in the British Islands,
(b) it is under the control of man whether on a permanent or temporary basis, or
(c) it is not living in a wild state.

3 Responsibility for animals

(1) In this Act, references to a person responsible for an animal are to a person responsible for an animal whether on a permanent or temporary basis.
(2) In this Act, references to being responsible for an animal include being in charge of it.
(3) For the purposes of this Act, a person who owns an animal shall always be regarded as being a person who is responsible for it.
(4) For the purposes of this Act, a person shall be treated as responsible for any animal for which a person under the age of 16 years of whom he has actual care and control is responsible.

4 Unnecessary suffering

(1) A person commits an offence if—
(a) an act of his, or a failure of his to act, causes an animal to suffer,
(b) he knew, or ought reasonably to have known, that the act, or failure to act, would have that effect or be likely to do so,
(c) the animal is a protected animal, and
(d) the suffering is unnecessary.
(2) A person commits an offence if—
(a) he is responsible for an animal,
(b) an act, or failure to act, of another person causes the animal to suffer,
(c) he permitted that to happen or failed to take such steps (whether by way of supervising the other person or otherwise) as were reasonable in all the circumstances to prevent that happening, and
(d) the suffering is unnecessary.
(3) The considerations to which it is relevant to have regard when determining for the purposes of this section whether suffering is unnecessary include—
(a) whether the suffering could reasonably have been avoided or reduced;
(b) whether the conduct which caused the suffering was in compliance with any relevant enactment or any relevant provisions of a licence or code of practice issued under an enactment;
(c) whether the conduct which caused the suffering was for a legitimate purpose, such as—
(i) the purpose of benefiting the animal, or
(ii) the purpose of protecting a person, property or another animal;
(d) whether the suffering was proportionate to the purpose of the conduct concerned;
(e) whether the conduct concerned was in all the circumstances that of a reasonably competent and humane person.

[F1 (3A) In determining for the purposes of subsection (1) whether suffering is unnecessary in a case where it was caused by conduct for a purpose mentioned in subsection (3)(c)(ii), the fact that the conduct was for that purpose is to be disregarded if—
(a) the animal was under the control of a relevant officer at the time of the conduct,

(b) it was being used by that officer at that time, in the course of the officer's duties, in a way that was reasonable in all the circumstances, and
(c) that officer is not the defendant.

(3B) In subsection (3A) 'relevant officer' means—
(a) a constable;
(b) a person (other than a constable) who has the powers of a constable or is otherwise employed for police purposes or is engaged to provide services for police purposes;
(c) a prisoner custody officer within the meaning of Part 4 of the Criminal Justice Act 1991.

(3C) The Secretary of State may by regulations amend subsection (3B). Only a person in the public service of the Crown may be specified in subsection (3B) by virtue of regulations under this subsection.**]**

(4) Nothing in this section applies to the destruction of an animal in an appropriate and humane manner.

Textual amendments

F1 S. 4(3A)-(3C) inserted (8.6.2019) by Animal Welfare (Service Animals) Act 2019 (c. 15), ss. 1(2), 2(2)

62 General interpretation

(1) In this Act—
'animal' has the meaning given by section 1(1);
'appropriate national authority' means—
(a) in relation to England, the Secretary of State;
(b) in relation to Wales, the National Assembly for Wales;
'enactment' includes an enactment contained in subordinate legislation (within the meaning of the Interpretation Act 1978 (c. 30));
'licence' means a licence for the purposes of section 13;
'local authority' means—
(a) in relation to England, a county council, a district council, a London borough council, the Common Council of the City of London or the Council of the Isles of Scilly;
(b) in relation to Wales, a county council or a county borough council;
'premises' includes any place and, in particular, includes—
(a) any vehicle, vessel, aircraft or hovercraft;
(b) any tent or movable structure;
'protected animal' has the meaning given by section 2;
'suffering' means physical or mental suffering and related expressions shall be construed accordingly;
'veterinary surgeon' means a person registered in the register of veterinary surgeons, or the supplementary veterinary register, kept under the Veterinary Surgeons Act 1966 (c. 36).

(2) In this Act, references to the occupier of premises, in relation to any vehicle, vessel, aircraft or hovercraft, are to the person who appears to be in charge of the vehicle, vessel, aircraft or hovercraft, and 'unoccupied' shall be construed accordingly.

(3) In this Act, references to a part of premises which is used as a private dwelling include any yard, garden, garage or outhouse which is used for purposes in connection with it.

(4) In this Act, references to responsibility, in relation to an animal, are to be read in accordance with section 3.

(5) In this Act, references to the needs of an animal are to be read in accordance with section 9(2).

(6) In this Act, references to a 'relevant post-conviction power' are to a power conferred by—
(a) section 33, 34, 37 or 42 of this Act,
(b) section 4(2) of the Performing Animals (Regulation) Act 1925 (c. 38) (power to remove name from register under Act and disqualify from registration),
(c) section 5(3) of the Pet Animals Act 1951 (c. 35) (power to cancel licence under Act and disqualify from carrying on licensable activity),
(d) section 3(3) of the Animal Boarding Establishments Act 1963 (c. 43) (provision corresponding to that mentioned in paragraph (c) above),
(e) section 4(3) of the Riding Establishments Act 1964 (c. 70) (further corresponding provision),
(f) section 3(4) of the Guard Dogs Act 1975 (c. 50) (power to cancel licence under Act),
(g) section 6(2) of the Dangerous Wild Animals Act 1976 (c. 38) (power to cancel licence under Act and disqualify from carrying on licensable activity), or
(h) section 4(4) of the Zoo Licensing Act 1981 (c. 37) (power to refuse licence under Act for conviction for an offence).

* * *

Source 2

Bandeira and Brannigan v RSPCA [2000] CO 2066/99

2. That section, which has been amended many times over the years and has become really rather unwieldy, now reads as follows:

> 'If any person shall cruelly beat, kick, ill-treat, override, overdrive, overload, torture, infuriate or terrify any animal or shall cause or procure or, being the owner, permit any animal to be so used or shall by wantonly or unreasonably doing or omitting to do any act or causing or procuring the commission or omission of any act, cause any unnecessary suffering or being the owner permit any unnecessary suffering to be so caused to any animal, he shall be guilty of an offence.'

. . .

5. What then are the facts of the case upon which the Magistrates found the offence proved?

They say this in paragraph 4 of the case:

(i) On the afternoon of Sunday 16 November 1997 the Appellants . . . were on the bank of the River Tees at Thornby. They had 3 dogs with them. They had 2 spades, some purse nets and an electronic ferret finder, which is attached to a dog and used to track its position underground.
(ii) [They found that the farmer had] no problem with foxes, which he liked . . .
(iii) [They found] in the vicinity of a badger set the Appellants . . . dug a large hole in the field. It was about 2 yards in diameter and at least 6 feet deep. They put the purse nets over holes in the river bank which were part of the badger set. They repeatedly put the dogs down the hole. At one point the Appellant Brannigan was suspended upside down in the hole by his ankles by the others while holding a dog.
(iv) The Appellants . . . were using the dogs to try and catch a badger or a fox. Although there was the scent of a fox at the badger set we were of the

opinion that they were seeking a badger because of its value in the practice of badger baiting.

(v) When the Lakeland terrier dog [the subject of the informations] was down the hole it was confronted by a badger or a fox. It had no room for manoeuvre. The badger and the fox are both larger than the dog, have sharp teeth and powerful claws. The dog suffered multiple lacerations to its face, nose, lips and mouth . . . its left upper incisor tooth was torn out.

. . .

7. They posed the following question for the opinion of this Court:

> 'Is a person who deliberately puts a dog into a set or earth or other habitation of a larger and more powerful wild animal which cannot escape and which is likely to and does cause injury to the dog, without lawful justification or excuse, guilty of cruelly ill-treating the dog under section 1(1)(a) of the Protection of Animals Act 1911?'

8. Mr Kilgour, who appears for the Appellants, says that dogs get themselves into all sorts of scraps – animals indulge in all sorts of activities, involving hunting, the Grand National and in a variety of other ways, all of which are activities which may, in certain circumstances, cause injury to the animal. He says it is wrong for the law to leave a wide spectrum of uncertainty as to what amounts to ill-treatment and what can be described as causing unnecessary suffering and suchlike, because this leaves the citizen with no idea of where he stands. He says, that the physical act, in which these two Appellants were engaged, amounted to no more than putting a dog's nose and feet at the beginning of a hole in the countryside, that dogs are always sniffing about doing things and, of course, may injure themselves, but that this cannot possibly be described as cruel ill-treatment.
9. As it seems to me, these questions are very much ones of fact for the Magistrates to decide. Life in the countryside is full of a whole variety of activities. Whether any particular thing amounts to ill-treatment in particular circumstances, whether or not it is unnecessary and whether or not any suffering which has been suffered by the animal has been caused by a human, is very much a question of fact for the Magistrates.
10. I would reject the submission of Mr Kilgour that if there is merely the risk that the animal will suffer injury, then it cannot be said that the human being has caused that animal unnecessary suffering, or can be regarded as ill-treating it.
11. As it seems to me, if the risk of injury is very high, then a finding of causation by the Magistrates is very likely. If the risk of injury is very low, then a finding of no causation by the Magistrates is very likely. One can conceive of circumstances where Magistrates arrive at a decision which is perverse. There is a spectrum or continuum between these two extremes and, no doubt there will be a position on that continuum where it is very difficult to say the one or the other. However, on the facts of the present case as set out in the Case Stated, and as I have read it, I see no problem at all about the finding to which the Crown Court came. It was open to them; it betrays no error of law, and I would dismiss this appeal.
12. MR JUSTICE ASTILL: I agree. I add only this so as to emphasise what my Lord has said. This decision should not be used generally as a flag to wave at those who hunt with dogs or any other animals. The Crown Court question was set, having regard to the facts that are peculiar to this case, and it is those facts that are the basis for this decision.

* * *

Source 3

DM [2023] EWCA Crim 150

1. We make an order under section 45 of the Youth Justice and Criminal Evidence Act 1999 by which no matter relating to either of two child victims concerned may be published that would identify them, including their name, address, any educational establishment, work place they attend or any picture of them. This order lasts until each child concerned reaches the age of 18.
2. On 24 May 2021, having pleaded guilty before the Liverpool magistrates' Court, the appellant was committed for sentence to Liverpool Crown Court for two offences of child neglect, contrary to section 1(1) of the Children and Young Persons Act 1933, and six offences of causing unnecessary suffering to a protected animal, contrary to sections 4(1) and 32(1) of the Animal Welfare Act 2006.
3. On 15 July 2022 the appellant was sentenced to a total of three years' imprisonment, comprising concurrent sentences of 2 years' imprisonment for each of the child neglect offences and 12 months' imprisonment for each offence of causing unnecessary suffering to a protected animal, those sentences to run concurrently with each other but consecutively to the 2 years' imprisonment imposed for the child neglect offences. Ancillary orders were made. The appellant now appeals those sentences by leave of the single judge.
4. The appellant and her two young children, aged [an age] and [an age], lived at an address in Birkenhead. On 19 November 2021 police attended that address as a result of concerns raised by neighbours. The police forced entry to the property which contained a number of dogs and was in a squalid state. There was no electricity, and dog faeces, human waste and rubbish was spread throughout the property. In the front room were several large dog cages piled with urine-soaked bedding and large piles of dog faeces were located throughout the room. There were faeces and blood on the kitchen floor. An upstairs child's room had a dog cage inside with dirty bedding. On the single bed were piles of fresh faeces. The bath was full of clothes and could not be used for washing. The appellant's bedroom, which was the cleanest room in the house, had a double bed and a dog cage with dirty bedding inside. The neglect to the appellant's two children was based on them living in these squalid conditions.
5. There were six dogs at the property, five of which were malnourished and in a poor state of health. There was no evidence of food or water available for them. A sixth dog was being eaten whilst still alive by two other dogs. That dog had bites on its face and muzzle, wounds across its body, torn skin near the stomach, one of its ears was missing and its organs were exposed. As a result of the level of injuries suffered, the dog had to be euthanized. The other five dogs were successfully treated and re-homed.
6. The appellant returned to the address whilst the officers were present and was arrested. Following her arrest, the appellant's [an age] daughter went to live with her father and the appellant's [an age] son was placed in local authority foster care. He was found to have an iron deficiency and was borderline anaemic. At the date of sentencing, it was reported that both children were now thriving and happy. There had been no contact between the children and the appellant since her arrest.

...

15. Turning to the remaining offences, prior to 29 June 2021, the maximum penalty for an offence of causing unnecessary suffering to an animal was six months. The maximum penalty for offences committed from that date has been increased to 5 years. The relevant sentencing guideline has not yet been amended to take account of the statutory changes, however, interim guidance has been produced which states that pending publication of a revised guideline:

> 'Courts may continue to refer to the existing guideline to assist in the assessment of the level of seriousness of the case, but the sentencing table will be of limited use in determining the sentence.'

On the existing guideline, a case in which there has been prolonged neglect, causing death, serious injury or a high level of suffering will fall into the top category for both culpability and harm. Offence 8, which related to the dog that was being eaten alive and later had to be euthanized as a result of its injuries, clearly falls into this category, which has a starting point of 18 weeks and a range of 12 to 26 weeks.

* * *

Source 4

Gray v RSPCA [2013] EWHC 500 (Admin)

Question 1: interpretation of 'knew or ought reasonably to have known' in section 4(1)(b)

24. The expression 'knew or ought reasonably to have known' is a common expression in English law and does not require to be glossed. A person who is responsible for an animal carries out the physical element (actus reus) of an offence under section 4(1) if he causes the animal to suffer unnecessarily, whether by act or omission. For the conduct to constitute an offence, the prosecution has to prove additionally that the defendant knew or ought to have known that his act or omission would, or was likely to, have that consequence. (To digress for a moment, it could be argued as a matter of strict grammar that the prosecution need only prove that the defendant knew or ought reasonably to have known that the act or omission would cause the animal to suffer, and not that the suffering would be unnecessary. That linguistic argument could be advanced because the 'knew or ought reasonably to have known' requirement is placed between paragraph (a) (causation of suffering) and (b) (unnecessary nature of the suffering), whereas paragraph (d) should more appropriately have come after paragraph (a) and before paragraph (b). However, it cannot have been the legislature's intention to criminalise an act done with realisation that it would cause the animal pain but in the honest and reasonable, albeit mistaken, belief that it was necessary for the animal's welfare. In the present case the judge directed himself that the prosecution had to establish that the defendant knew or ought reasonably to have known both that his or her act or failure would cause an animal to suffer and that the suffering was unnecessary. In my judgment he was right.)

25. Mr Fullerton submitted on Mr Michael Gray's behalf that, on its proper construction, section 4(1)(b) requires either proof of knowledge that the animal was in a condition causing it unnecessary suffering or proof that it was showing signs of suffering which could not be missed by a reasonable, caring owner. The effect of his submission was that the offence requires either actual knowledge or a form of constructive knowledge that the animal was showing signs of unnecessary suffering, and that negligence is not sufficient.
26. That submission does not accord with a natural reading of the language of the subsection. Its plain effect is to impose criminal liability for unnecessary suffering caused to an animal either by an act or omission which the person responsible knew would, or was likely to, cause unnecessary suffering, or by a negligent act or omission.
27. In support of his argument Mr Fullerton relied on authorities relating to section 1(1)(a) of the Protection of Animals Act 1911. That provision made it an offence if a person:

> shall cruelly beat, kick, ill-treat, over-ride, over-drive, over-load, torture, infuriate, or terrify any animal, or shall cause or procure, or, being the owner, permit any animal to be so used, or shall, by wantonly or unreasonably doing or omitting to do any act, or causing or procuring the commission or omission of any act, cause any unnecessary suffering, or, being the owner, permit any unnecessary suffering to be so caused to any animal.

28. That Act was the corner piece of animal welfare legislation prior to its repeal and replacement by the 2006 Act. The judge took the view that the language of section 1(1)(a) of the 1911 Act, and authorities as to its construction, were irrelevant to the construction of section 4 of the 2006 Act. The judge was right. The language of the provisions is significantly different. It would be wrong in principle to construe the provisions of the 2006 Act by reference to differently worded provisions of the repealed legislation.
29. Further, if there were ambiguity about section 4(1) of the 2006 Act (which is not the case), the Explanatory Notes, the departmental select committee's report and the Government's response to that report make it clear that the offence was intended to capture unnecessary suffering caused by negligence. The committee's recommendation 17 included:

> the mens rea element of the clause 1(1) cruelty offence [which became section 4 in the 2006 Act] should be assessed by means of an objective test, so that the defendant's conduct will be assessed on the basis of what a reasonable person in the position of the defendant would have known about the consequences of his or her conduct.

30. The Government stated in its reply:

> The cruelty offence was always intended to capture acts of neglect where these amounted to unnecessary suffering... We agree with the comments regarding the mens rea element and an objective mental test will apply, ie knew or ought reasonably to have known.

* * *

Source 5

Reproduced by permission of RELX (UK) Limited, trading as LexisNexis.

Halsbury's Laws of England > Animals (Volume 2 (2023)) > 5. Animal Welfare and Protection from Cruelty > (2) Animal Welfare under the Animal Welfare Act 2006 > (iii) Prevention of Harm to Animals

144 Intention and cruelty

Except for the offence of administering poison and certain offences relating to animal fights, the Animal Welfare Act 2006 does not expressly refer to wilfulness or intention in the mind of the offender, and the offences which it creates consist in the doing of forbidden acts or causing or permitting them to be done with the qualification, in the case of causing suffering, that the suffering is unnecessary. Thus, in general, an intention to commit cruelty need not be proved. On the other hand, if the charge is of causing or permitting an act to be done, guilty knowledge must be shown, or the causing or procuring will not be proved.

The meaning of the adverb 'cruelly' has never been expressly defined in legislation. Under the nineteenth century legislation, it was taken to mean 'the unnecessary abuse of any animal', and this interpretation has been endorsed. By the beginning of the twentieth century it appeared to have been established that 'cruelty' had the meaning not only of cruel in the sense of paining the animal, but cruel in the sense that it is unnecessary. The courts have continued to apply this established interpretation, suggesting that the word 'cruelly' could not be better defined than 'causing unnecessary suffering'. The Animal Welfare Act 2006 does not use the words 'cruel' or 'cruelty', but instead refers to 'suffering'.

146 Causing unnecessary suffering

A person commits an offence if:

(1) an act of theirs, or a failure of theirs to act, causes an animal to suffer;
(2) he knew, or ought reasonably to have known, that the act, or failure to act, would have that effect or be likely to do so;
(3) the animal is a protected animal; and
(4) the suffering is unnecessary.

A person commits an offence if:
(a) he is responsible for an animal;
(b) an act, or failure to act, of another person causes the animal to suffer;
(c) he permitted that to happen or failed to take such steps (whether by way of supervising the other person or otherwise) as were reasonable in all the circumstances to prevent that happening; and
(d) the suffering is unnecessary.

* * *

Source 6

Isted v Crown Prosecution Service [1998] 162 JP 513

Mr Justice Gage: . . . On 21 April 1996, the date of the alleged offence, Jason Parker discovered Lily in the pig pen on the Appellant's land. Lily was about a metre or a metre and a half away from a pig's face with teeth bared and barking. Mr Parker shouted at Lily but to no effect. Mr Parker reported the incident to the Appellant. What happened next is set out at paragraph J of the Case:

> 'Mr Isted went straight to the gun cabinet. He collected his shotgun. The cartridges used were in fact small sized cartridges designed for shooting rabbits or pheasants. Mr Isted accepted he should have picked up a larger shot. He proceeded to the pen. He made no attempt to drive the dog away. From twenty yards he opened fire. The shot peppered Lily's head. She yelped and ran off. Lily was seen limping by Mrs Helena Lang, a neighbour, as she made her way back to Mrs Ewen.'

The dog survived the shooting and returned to Mrs Ewen. She was clearly injured. In the course of this appeal a point was taken on behalf of the Appellant that evidence from a veterinary surgeon about injuries sustained by the dog was not properly admitted by the Justices. This point was not raised either in the Magistrates Court or in the Case. It was not pursued before us by Counsel with any vigour, in my view rightly. It is perfectly clear that even in the absence of evidence from a veterinary surgeon the Justices would have been quite entitled to infer that the injuries to Lily caused by the shooting and seen by Mrs Ewen had also caused suffering to Lily.

On these facts the Justices convicted the appellant. The first question in the Case for this Court is whether on the evidence the Justices were entitled to find that it was not reasonably necessary for the appellant to shoot Lily. There are other questions raised in the Case but the principle point taken on this appeal by the Appellant is that the Justices wrongly convicted him of the offence because he was doing no more than was reasonably necessary to protect his pig.

. . .

It is agreed by both Counsel that the Court is solely concerned with the question of the reasonableness or otherwise of the Appellant's action. In the case the Justices refer to the advice received by them from their clerk, which was based on the case of *Barnard v Evans* [1925] 2 KB 794. That advice was that they should ask themselves the question:

> 'Whether there was any reasonable necessity to shoot the dog in order to drive it away?'

Neither Counsel challenge that as the correct test to be applied in this case. It is also agreed by Counsel that the Justices were correct to reject an argument placed before them on behalf of the Appellant that the Appellant was entitled to raise a defence provided by Section 9 of the Animals Act 1971. Accordingly the sole question in this appeal is whether on the evidence the magistrates were entitled to hold that it was not reasonably necessary for the Appellant to shoot Lily.

Before turning to the detailed facts found by the Justices and their opinion on that issue I must deal with a further point raised in the course of this appeal but not before the Justices. Initially counsel for the Respondent, Mr James Cooper, submitted that in deciding the question of reasonable necessity the Justices should view what the Appellant did objectively but taking into account facts which he knew to be true but not matters which he believed to be true but were not true. Mr Simon Medland, appearing on behalf of the Appellant, contended that the test to be applied was the more conventional test namely that the justices should decide whether what the appellant did was reasonable based on their objective assessment of his actions in the light of the facts and circumstances at the time, as the Appellant genuinely believed them to be. In my judgment, Mr Medland's submissions on this point are to be preferred. In written submissions invited by the court following oral argument, Mr Cooper indicated that he was prepared to concede that his submission on this point was wrong. As it happens, the difference is not of any real significance in this appeal.

Mr Medland's first submission on the main point was that although the Justices were given the correct advice by their clerk they failed to apply that advice correctly to the facts as they found them. He pointed to a number of passages in the Case which appeared to conflict with the Justices' stated finding that it was not reasonably necessary for the Appellant to shoot the dog. In particular Mr Medland relied on three short passages from the Case.

They were:

> 'We found that the dog Lily suffered as a result of Mr Isted shooting her because she was not shot and killed immediately or outright';
>
> 'We found this suffering was unnecessary because she was not killed outright, by the single shot, but left in this state.';
>
> 'Had the dog been killed and had there been evidence to show that she had not suffered unnecessarily we would not have found the case proved under Section 1(1) of the Protection of Animals Act 1911. This was not the case on the evidence.'

Mr Medland submitted, with some force, that the Justices appear to have concluded that if the dog had been killed outright no offence would have been committed. He submitted that such a conclusion could only be reached upon the basis that they found that it was reasonably necessary for him to shoot to kill the dog.

. . .

Mr Medland's second point was that the Justices' finding was wrong on the facts of the case and judged against the background known to the Appellant. He submitted that judged against the background of dogs roaming onto his property and Lily's earlier excursion when chasing geese, the Appellant was quite entitled to take up his shotgun and shoot Lily when the dog was on the point of attacking his pig. In my judgment, the difficulty with this submission is that that was a matter for the Justices to decide and they decided it adversely to the Appellant. Others might have taken a different view but, in my judgment, on the evidence before them, the Justices cannot be said to have reached a conclusion which no Justices directing themselves properly and taking into account all the evidence, could have reached. In my view that submission fails as well.

Accordingly, I answer the questions in the Case as follows:

1. Yes;
2. They were correct in ruling that section 9 of the Animals Act 1971 was not relevant;

. . .

In my view the appeal must be dismissed.

Lord Justice Brooke:

I agree, and I am only adding a few words of my own because the present state of the law is so unnecessarily confusing.

The magistrates were quite right not to be beguiled by a submission that the defence which is afforded in civil proceedings by Section 9 of the Animals Act 1971 has no relevance in criminal proceedings. That Act is based on the draft Bill annexed to the Law Commission's Report on Civil Liability for Animals (1967) Law Com No 13, and the Law Commission said in terms that in their opinion it would be inadvisable to deal with criminal charges, where different considerations might apply, in the context of that report, and that the matter would be better considered as part of a general review of the law relating to malicious damage (ibid, p 38, footnote 142).

The Law Commission returned to this topic in its Report on Offences of Damage to Property (1970) Law Com No 29. The Criminal Damage Act 1971 is based on the draft Bill annexed to this Report. The relevant passage of the report is at pp 18–20, and what has emerged in legislative form is the defence which is available in Section 5(2) of the 1971 Act. Thus if someone intentionally or recklessly (see s 1(1)) destroys or damages a dog belonging to another (a dog being property within the meaning of the Act: see s 10(1)), he will be treated for the purposes of the Act as having a lawful excuse if he did this act 'in order to protect property belonging to himself or another . . . and at the time of the act or acts alleged to constitute the offence he believed—

(i) that the property . . . was in immediate need of protection; and
(ii) that the means of protection adopted . . . were . . . reasonable having regard to all the circumstances' (see s 5(2)(b)).

It is expressly provided that for the purposes of Section 5 it is immaterial whether a belief is justified if it is honestly held. Compare Miles v Hutchings [1903] 2 KB 714 per Channell J at p 717.

If in the present case the Appellant had killed Mrs Ewen's dog, he would have been liable to be convicted of an offence under Section 1(1) of the Criminal Damage Act 1971, and the Justices would no doubt have had to consider the language of Section 5 of that Act when determining, to the criminal standard of proof, whether he shot and killed the dog without lawful excuse. For my part, I agree with them that they could not have convicted him of an offence under Section 1(1) of the 1911 Act if the dog had been killed outright in circumstances where she did not suffer unnecessarily.

This appeal has highlighted an anomaly in the law, since the requisite mental element for an offence under the 1971 Act is framed in modern intelligible language of a type which the Law Commission is now urging the Government to introduce into our legislation for offences against the person, while the relevant part of Section 1(1) of the Protection of Animals Act 1911 is framed by reference to the antique law underlying words like 'wantonly or unreasonably' which is bound to go on giving trouble to those concerned with the administration of the law.

Indeed, since there can be no doubt that the appellant intentionally damaged Lily, he could have been charged with an offence contrary to Section 1 of the Criminal Damage Act 1971 where the test of the mental element is different and the concept of a 'lawful excuse' phrased in intelligible language which is more generous to a defendant.

While I am not suggesting that where the suffering of animals is in question the less generous policy articulated in the 1911 Act is not a reasonable one, it would in

> my judgment be desirable for the Law Commission to consider, when its resources permit, the relationship between the 1911 Act and the 1971 Act where damage to people's animals is in question. Even if the policy of the law may be different in cases of damage to animate property, it is surely high time that that policy was expressed [in] clear, intelligible modern language, which would avoid all the unnecessary legal expenditure that currently has to be devoted to cases like this.
>
> . . . For the reasons set out in the judgment of the court, copies of which have been made available to both parties, this appeal is dismissed.
>
>

* * *

■ YOUR TURN

Have a go at answering question 1, remembering the guidance on page 22.

- Refer to the structured approach in the SRA's assessment criteria on page 23.
- Conduct focused legal research of the question by carefully reading the primary sources (case law and legislation) and secondary sources (published works that commentate on the law).
- When assessing whether or not a source is relevant, ask yourself: does it deal with the same type of offence as the question? Does it interpret a provision of the Act that you are dealing with? Is it found on the same or similar facts, and is that authority binding?
- List all relevant issues which you will discuss and any issues that arise.
- Provide a concise and well-reasoned analysis based on your research, avoiding too much jargon and complexity.
- Timings are important: you will need to prepare and write your answer in 60 minutes. Be mindful of how long you want to spend reading the sources provided, writing your answer and then reviewing it.

SQE1 Functioning legal knowledge link
Remember chapter 1 of ***Revise SQE: Criminal Law***, where the general principles of criminal law were considered. As you might not have covered the specifics of the offences that you face in your legal research assessment task, it is important that you familiarise yourself with those general concepts.

EVALUATING YOUR ANSWER

When you have attempted question 1, mark it yourself against the SQE2 legal research assessment criteria. Do you think your attempt met the threshold standard?

Now compare your attempt with the following key legal points and two sample answers to the question. A circled number indicates that commentary is provided for this part of the answer. The commentary explains whether or not the sample answer satisfies the assessment criteria and is likely to meet the SQE2 threshold standard.

➥Key legal points: question 1

In this assessment, part or all of the following sources are relevant to the question:

- Animal Welfare Act 2006, ss 1–4, 62
- *Gray v RSPCA* [2013] EWHC 500 (Admin)
- *Halsbury's Laws of England*, Animals, vol. 2, paras 144, 146
- *Isted v Crown Prosecution Service* [1998] 162 JP 513.

The following sources are not relevant to the question:

- *Bandeira and Brannigan v RSPCA* [2000] CO 2066/99
- *DM* [2023] EWCA Crim 150.

Key legal points include the following:

- The key question here is whether the acts that James committed amounted to unnecessary suffering under the Act.
- The relevant sources define the offence and give an interpretation of the requirements of the offence. *Gray v RSPCA* stipulates that a person may be liable if they knew or ought reasonably to have known their act would cause suffering. *Isted v CPS* confirms that the reasonableness of the actions is essential. These are the key points that you are being asked to assess here.
- Note that the irrelevant sources use old legislation. For example, *Bandeira and Brannigan v RSPCA* deals with the Protection of Animals Act 1911 and not the 2006 Act.
- The offence of causing unnecessary suffering is contained within s 4(1) Animal Welfare Act 2006 and there is an aid to interpretation within ss 4(3) and 62(1) of the same Act. In essence, a person commits an offence where a person responsible for a protected animal, either by an act or omission, causes an animal to suffer unnecessarily, and they know or ought to know that said act or omission would cause an animal to suffer unnecessarily.
- The elements of the offence are set out in two parts: first, the act or omission that causes unnecessary suffering; second, the mental element of knowing or being ought to know that it would cause the unnecessary suffering.
- There is no issue with the definition that both Alpha and Bravo are protected animals for which the client was responsible. A 'protected animal' is defined in s 2 Animal Welfare Act 2006 and is summarised as an animal that is commonly domesticated in the British Islands, is under the control of man or is not living in a wild state.
- In relation to Alpha, there is no offence, following from the logic in *Isted v CPS*; it can be surmised from that judgment that there is no offence when an animal is killed immediately or outright. In this case it is clear from the facts the client has provided (and hence the evidence that would likely come out at trial) that Alpha died immediately; therefore, there was no 'suffering' within the meaning of the Act. As a result, there can be no offence. The client should plead not guilty to the charge relating to Alpha.
- The position in relation to Bravo is less straightforward. Here, the question of whether there was suffering and, if so, whether it was unnecessary, must be considered. As mentioned, it is essentially a two-stage test.
- As to whether there was suffering, it is undoubtedly clear that there was. Bravo suffered a fractured skull and a bleed on his brain, and he remains in intensive care. Following s 62 of the 2006 Act, 'suffering' means physical or mental suffering, and related expressions shall be construed accordingly. Though case law provided in the sources explains this concept further, it is clear that the injuries suffered by Bravo, and his awareness of them (the whimpering), meet the statutory threshold.

- The final question in respect of Bravo is whether or not the suffering was necessary. The relevant law is contained within s 4(3) of the 2006 Act. The two kicks to Bravo were in order to prevent injury to a dog who was clearly deceased, or to prevent damage to the dog's remains. It is submitted that there were other means of achieving this aim (grabbing the collar, pushing, shouting or even (arguably) a single kick to the body rather than two, and at least only one to the head). Considering the factors in s 4(3)(a–e), it is likely the suffering would be considered unnecessary. On that basis, the client may wish to give careful thought to pleading guilty to the charge in relation to Bravo. That decision remains, of course, one for the client.

SAMPLE ANSWER 1 TO QUESTION 1

I have reviewed the details of James's case regarding the charges under s 4(1) of the Animal Welfare Act 2006. In short, I consider a not-guilty plea in respect of Alpha but a guilty plea in respect of Bravo to be appropriate. Please find below a summary of my research. ❶

The key issue in this case is whether James's actions towards his dogs, Alpha and Bravo, caused unnecessary suffering within the meaning of the Animal Welfare Act 2006. Section 4(1) of the Act states that a person responsible for a protected animal commits an offence if they cause unnecessary suffering to that animal by an act or omission, whilst knowing (or being ought to know) that such an act or omission would cause suffering. ❷

Regarding Alpha ❸

It seems clear that no offence has occurred. From the facts, it is apparent that Alpha died instantly from the gunshot to the head. In situations where an animal dies immediately, no offence under s 4(1) of the Animal Welfare Act arises. This follows the decision in *Isted v Crown Prosecution Service* [1998] 162 JP 513, ❹ which (although in relation to an earlier form of the offence) ❺ held that, as an instantaneous death by its nature involves no suffering, no offence can occur when an animal is killed instantly: 'Had the dog been killed and had there been evidence to show that she had not suffered unnecessarily we would not have found the case proved under Section 1(1) of the Protection of Animals Act 1911.' Therefore, there is no basis for the charge relating to Alpha. I would recommend advising James to plead not guilty to this charge.

Regarding Bravo

The situation with Bravo is more complex. There is no doubt that Bravo suffered significant injury, including a fractured skull and a brain bleed, and was likely aware of those injuries (the whimpering). Under s 62(1) of the Animal Welfare Act, 'suffering' is defined to include both physical and mental suffering. The injuries sustained by Bravo, coupled with the whimpering he exhibited, make it clear that both physical and mental suffering occurred. ❻

The next issue to consider is whether the suffering inflicted on Bravo was unnecessary. Section 4(3)(a–e) of the Act assists here: the court would have regard to, in this case, (a) whether the suffering could reasonably have been avoided or reduced, (c) whether the conduct served a legitimate purpose, (d) proportionality and (e) whether 'the conduct concerned was in all the circumstances that of a reasonably competent and humane person'. ❼

James states that he kicked Bravo to move him off Alpha's body. However, other methods could have been employed to achieve the same outcome, such as using

Bravo's collar to pull him away or issuing a command. Additionally, one kick might have been sufficient, rather than two, particularly as these were kicks to the head. The fact that James administered two kicks to Bravo's head raises concerns about whether the suffering was necessary. *Gray v RSPCA* [2013] EWHC 500 (Admin) interprets s 4(3) of the Animal Welfare Act 2006 and confirms that the considerations are not exhaustive but provide a framework for assessing whether suffering was necessary. It is likely in this situation that the court would conclude that, even though the suffering may have served a legitimate purpose (protection of property), it could also have been avoided and was neither proportionate nor reasonable. ❽

Therefore, I would consider that the offence under s 4(1) for Bravo has a stronger basis than the charge for Alpha and is likely to be made out at any trial.

Recommendation

In summary, I do not believe James has committed an offence in relation to Alpha, because the facts suggest that no unnecessary suffering occurred. As such, I recommend advising James to plead not guilty to the charge concerning Alpha.

With respect to Bravo, however, the unnecessary suffering caused by the two kicks to the head suggest that James has committed the s 4(1) offence. I would advise James to carefully consider pleading guilty to the charge related to Bravo. However, the decision on how to plead is ultimately for James to make. ❾

Please let me know if I can be of any further assistance, in this or indeed any other matter.

COMMENTARY

❶ This introductory paragraph is useful to the reader, both the fictitious partner and the real SQE2 assessor: it foreshadows the candidate's conclusions and introduces their research journey there. This immediately provides a clear and practical summary of the findings in a concise manner, which is good practice.

❷ Setting out the issues in the question is an excellent first step: without just regurgitating the offence itself, the candidate demonstrates that they can narrow their own research question based on information and sources available to them. This paragraph clearly articulates the legal test which is relevant to the issues at hand (act/omission; unnecessary suffering; knowledge or constructive knowledge) and explains the key provisions well. This shows a strong understanding of legal principles, which meets the SQE2's assessment criteria.

❸ The use of headings indicates a structured and logical approach to the answer. Including headings makes the advice more comprehensible for the assessor and easier to read, as it breaks the case into two separate analyses for each dog rather than bulking them together.

❹ Signposting and quoting from the sources provided in the question is a very good way for the candidate to show that they have appropriately considered the materials: remember that this assessment is about research, not your own legal knowledge. Even if the assessment question is on a topic that you are very knowledgeable about, make sure that you relate your answer to the sources provided so that you can demonstrate your research skills.

❺ By recognising limitations in the sources that they have selected, the candidate shows critical analysis and advanced thinking skills, both very important for legal research. The identification of *Isted v CPS* and the acknowledgement that it relates to an earlier version of the offence but is still relevant demonstrates good legal reasoning with application to the given facts.

6 This paragraph uses a fact-law-application approach to its structure. This is a particularly helpful approach to the SQE2 assessment as it shows that the candidate has taken one of the facts from the brief, used the research sources provided to apply the law to that fact and then formed a conclusion.

7 By selecting the relevant parts of a source rather than adopting the whole source, the candidate demonstrates that they can focus on relevance and quality rather than quantity and coverage. This is an important research skill and addresses the requirement of the assessment criteria to be client-focused.

8 This is a detailed part of the answer that stays close to the facts and uses interpretation effectively. The inclusion of *Gray v RSPCA* is suitable and directly relates to the point that the candidate is making. The tone is measured and avoids speculation, and as such satisfies the assessment criteria in making clear links between legal principles and how they may be applied in this case.

9 This is a nice ethical touch: the candidate has remembered that ethics are pervasive to SQE2 assessments. The candidate gives clear, client-focused advice about the strength of evidence whilst making it explicit that the ultimate decision rests with the client. This demonstrates an understanding of both professional integrity and the client's right to make informed decisions about their case, thus meeting two separate assessment criteria. Overall, the recommendation section directly addresses the key points (advice as to plea) that the partner will be considering at this stage of the litigation. The recommendations are helpfully made after a simple but thorough explanation of how the law applies to the facts in James's case.

Does this answer meet the threshold?

This answer is likely to meet the assessment criteria threshold. The candidate identifies and uses relevant source material provided, and makes only specific and necessary references to those parts of the source material. The answer does not cite all relevant sources (such as *Halsbury's Laws of England*), but, while this could increase marks for the candidate, it is not detrimental to their success in the exam. There is always room to improve with an assessment such as this; however, the answer as it currently stands would be suitable for a pass mark. The answer addresses the requirements in the assessment criteria to identify and use relevant sources, provide advice that is client-focused and apply the law correctly and comprehensively to the client's situation.

The answer discloses no critical misunderstandings and also demonstrates an ability to advise ethically. There is some missing information (such as James's legal responsibility for the dogs) and some use of informalities in the response, but neither of these points is critical to the answer's likely passing status. In the main the answer uses clear and acceptable language to meet the requirements of the assessment criteria.

Now consider the second sample answer to question 1.

■ SAMPLE ANSWER 2 TO QUESTION 1

I've gone through James's case and here's my take. The main thing to consider is if James caused unnecessary suffering, which would mean he's guilty of the offence under the Animal Welfare Act 2006. The key point is whether his actions caused suffering, and whether he knew or should've known that they would. 1

As for Alpha, the facts seem pretty clear. James says Alpha died instantly from the shot. Case law notes that when an animal dies immediately, there's no real 'suffering' involved. ❷ Since Alpha passed away right away, there doesn't appear to be any basis for the charge. It seems James should be pleading not guilty to this one, as no real suffering was caused.

On to Bravo, it's a bit trickier. ❸ It's clear Bravo was injured badly - fractured skull, bleeding and still in intensive care. So, there's no doubt he suffered both physically and mentally. But the question is, was it necessary? James says he kicked Bravo to move him off Alpha's body, but I'd argue there were other ways to do this without causing harm. For example, grabbing his collar or just moving him by hand, or even just a single kick rather than two. Kicking Bravo twice in the head seems a bit extreme, especially when there were probably other ways of moving him. ❹

The issue really is whether James could've avoided the suffering. He had other options, and it seems likely the two kicks to Bravo's head were unnecessary. So, there's a chance he's committed an offence here, even if his intention wasn't malicious - he ought to have known that his kicks would cause suffering. ❺

In conclusion, I don't think there's much of a case for Alpha. The facts suggest no suffering, so not guilty seems the way to go there. However, with Bravo, the suffering seems unnecessary, so James may want to consider pleading guilty to that charge, but that's for him to decide.

Let me know if you need more info or if you'd like to discuss things further. *Halsbury's Laws on Animals* was quite useful; you might want to read that. ❻

Best regards,

COMMENTARY

❶ The first thing to notice here is that the writing is not formal enough. Remember the requirements of the assessment criteria, to use clear, concise, precise, *acceptable* language: this paragraph (and in fact the whole response) is casually written. See point 3 below on this aspect too. For example, a phrase such as 'here's my take' is inappropriate for communicating with a partner. Try to avoid contractions in your answers too; the candidate would have made a better impression by writing 'I have' instead of 'I've' and 'he is' instead of 'he's'.

The second point is that the candidate has not identified that there are *two* charges, each relating to a different dog. This paragraph reads as though there is only one charge, which creates ambiguity and may mislead the assessor. The candidate should set out clearly that there are two potential offences and base their analysis on this structure. The paragraph implies that the candidate has failed to understand the case sufficiently; they will therefore be unable to apply the law correctly which in turn will make it impossible to give client-focused advice. The candidate will thus fail to meet the assessment criteria on two grounds.

❷ Reference to 'case law' does not sufficiently show that the candidate is referring to the sources provided with the question. It will be difficult for the assessor to satisfy themselves that the candidate has demonstrated their ability to use the sources which are relevant to inform their answer, as required by the assessment criteria. Without specifically citing a case, the persuasive nature of the point can be lost, and the answer does not demonstrate research skills adequately enough to achieve the SQE2 threshold.

❸ The use of informal language has its place, but this candidate overuses informality in this response to such an extent that it undermines the formality of the assessment task. A more nuanced, professional tone is required for this kind of communication and to meet the assessment criterion for acceptable language.

4 The candidate properly outlines elements of the test for whether suffering is necessary but fails to cite the relevant elements of the sources provided. This was a prime opportunity to reference s 4(3) Animal Welfare Act 2006, which specifically sets out the statutory test upon which the offence would be made out. Applying the legislation (and doing so correctly) is critical for fully developing the analysis in the SQE2 legal research assessment and meeting the assessment criteria.

5 The use of the word 'chance' in this paragraph will lead the assessor to doubt that the candidate holds an informed view based on the sources. In the assessment, you must decide and present an informed view based on the resources that you have been presented with, in order to give client-focused advice. Uncertainty and hesitation to commit to a conclusion suggest that the candidate is not confident in their own work. To demonstrate a solid understanding of the case and provide clear advice, the issues should be addressed from both sides, with the response taking a well-reasoned position rather than remaining neutral or indecisive.

6 In practice, referring someone to further sources can sometimes be useful, but in the SQE2 assessment you will be expected to read the sources carefully yourself and make a judgement on their relevance, not create more work for the partner. Here the candidate makes only a passing reference to the Halsbury's source (and cites the title inaccurately), which does not add much to the answer. It indicates that the candidate has perhaps skim-read the source and noticed that it might apply to this issue but is leaving it to the assessor to decide. Citing and applying a source which is relevant would gain the candidate marks as it indicates a clear understanding of the extract and its application to the fact pattern.

Does this answer meet the threshold?

This answer uses broadly the same structure, logic and sources as sample answer 1, but the candidate's research skills have not been demonstrated because the answer does not fully engage with the sources that have been provided. The candidate has not demonstrated that they can identify and use relevant sources and information, because they barely mention the sources and do not cite specific elements of those resources to reinforce their advice. They have not followed the partner's instructions to include legal reasoning and any key sources or authorities in their answer, which is an essential part of the SQE2 assessment. As also noted in the commentary, the writing style is too informal and does not meet the assessment criteria's requirements for 'clear, precise, concise and acceptable' language.

Therefore, even though this candidate reaches the same, correct conclusion as sample answer 1, sample answer 2 does not meet the specific assessment criteria for SQE2 legal research for the reasons outlined above and would not pass the threshold. Remember that for this assessment your answer must demonstrate that you can use the sources provided to answer the question fully.

Question 2 is based on a scenario commonly encountered by criminal practitioners - possession with intent to supply Class A drugs. You might encounter a problem like this in your SQE2 legal research assessment, where you are asked to apply your understanding of relevant legal principles, identify and analyse the appropriate sources and present a well-reasoned conclusion.

■ QUESTION 2

Email to candidate

From: Partner
Sent: 9 February 202#
To: Candidate
Subject: New client enquiry - Sarah Smith
A new client, Sarah, telephoned me this morning. She has been told she will be charged with possession with intent to supply a Class A drug.

The police attended an address in Colchester following an anonymous tip-off. Sarah was found inside the property, along with a large quantity of what appeared to be cocaine, some cash in small amounts and several unused snap bags. Sarah was in the property with two other individuals in the living room, sitting near the coffee table where most of the items were recovered.

Sarah told the police that the drugs were not hers and that she was only visiting the property to play video games with her friends. She denied any involvement in drug dealing and claimed not to know that the drugs were there. Sarah claims that she did not take anything with her to the property and had no intention of engaging in illegal activity.

Sarah has also queried whether a person can be guilty of possession with intent to supply if, on the facts, they were simply holding the drugs on behalf of someone else and they intended to give the drugs back to that same person.

Sarah was not charged at the station but has been told that a charge is imminent. One of the attending police officers described Sarah as 'twitchy, aggressive and clearly up to no good - she looked very disturbed'. Sarah is concerned about the prejudicial nature of this comment and its potential impact on the legality of the search and the fairness of a trial should this go to court.

Sarah has no previous convictions for drug offences but does have a caution for possession of cannabis from three years ago, when she was 19 years old.

Sarah would like to know whether, on these facts, the charge for possession with intent to supply is likely to be made out. Sarah would also like to know whether 'holding' the drugs for someone would amount to possession. If the charge is likely to be made out and she is found guilty, I would also like you to consider and address the potential sentencing outcomes.

Based on the information above and the sources provided, please research the answer to these questions. Please report back to me so that I can advise the client.

You should include, for my reference, your legal reasoning, mentioning any key sources or authorities.

Many thanks,

Partner.

Note to candidates:

Given the time constraints of this assessment, we have not provided the full text of some primary sources. For the purposes of this assessment, where the full text of a primary source is not provided, candidates may nevertheless cite the primary source

on the basis it is referred to in one or more of the secondary sources provided and the full text can be checked at a later date.

Information displayed is as obtained on the date of search, for example purposes only. Information herein is not to be relied upon outside the purposes of this sample question.

Attachments

You have been provided with the following sources listed alphabetically in order of source name. The order of presentation is not intended as a guide to the order in which they should be consulted.

PLEASE NOTE THAT PART OR ALL OF SOME OF THESE SOURCES MAY NOT BE RELEVANT TO ANSWERING THE QUESTION

1. Misuse of Drugs Act 1971 ss 4, 5, 28
2. Psychoactive Substances Act 2016 ss 2-7
3. *R v Lambert* [2001] UKHL 37
4. *R v Maginnis* [1987] AC 303
5. Sentencing Council Guidelines: Possession of a controlled drug
6. Sentencing Council Guidelines: Supplying or offering to supply a controlled drug/ Possession of a controlled drug with intent to supply it to another

* * *

Source 1

Misuse of Drugs Act 1971 ss 4, 5, 28

4 Restriction of production and supply of controlled drugs

(1) Subject to any regulations under section 7 of this Act, or any provision made in a temporary class drug order by virtue of section 7A, for the time being in force, it shall not be lawful for a person—
(a) to produce a controlled drug; or
(b) to supply or offer to supply a controlled drug to another.
(2) Subject to section 28 of this Act, it is an offence for a person—
(a) to produce a controlled drug in contravention of subsection (1) above; or
(b) to be concerned in the production of such a drug in contravention of that subsection by another.
(3) Subject to section 28 of this Act, it is an offence for a person—
(a) to supply or offer to supply a controlled drug to another in contravention of subsection (1) above; or
(b) to be concerned in the supplying of such a drug to another in contravention of that subsection; or
(c) to be concerned in the making to another in contravention of that subsection of an offer to supply such a drug.

5 Restriction of possession of controlled drugs

(1) Subject to any regulations under section 7 of this Act for the time being in force, it shall not be lawful for a person to have a controlled drug in his possession.

(2) Subject to section 28 of this Act and to subsection (4) below, it is an offence for a person to have a controlled drug in his possession in contravention of subsection (1) above.

(2A) Subsections (1) and (2) do not apply in relation to a temporary class drug.

(3) Subject to section 28 of this Act, it is an offence for a person to have a controlled drug in his possession, whether lawfully or not, with intent to supply it to another in contravention of section 4(1) of this Act.

(4) In any proceedings for an offence under subsection (2) above in which it is proved that the accused had a controlled drug in his possession, it shall be a defence for him to prove—

(a) that, knowing or suspecting it to be a controlled drug, he took possession of it for the purpose of preventing another from committing or continuing to commit an offence in connection with that drug and that as soon as possible after taking possession of it he took all such steps as were reasonably open to him to destroy the drug or to deliver it into the custody of a person lawfully entitled to take custody of it; or

(b) that, knowing or suspecting it to be a controlled drug, he took possession of it for the purpose of delivering it into the custody of a person lawfully entitled to take custody of it and that as soon as possible after taking possession of it he took all such steps as were reasonably open to him to deliver it into the custody of such a person.

(5) Subsection (4) above shall apply in the case of proceedings for an offence under section 19(1) of this Act consisting of an attempt to commit an offence under subsection (2) above as it applies in the case of proceedings for an offence under subsection (2), subject to the following modifications, that is to say—

(a) for the references to the accused having in his possession, and to his taking possession of, a controlled drug there shall be substituted respectively references to his attempting to get, and to his attempting to take, possession of such a drug; and

(b) in paragraphs (a) and (b) the words from 'and that as soon as possible' onwards shall be omitted.

(6) Nothing in subsection (4) or (5) above shall prejudice any defence which it is open to a person charged with an offence under this section to raise apart from that subsection.

28 Proof of lack of knowledge etc. to be a defence in proceedings for certain offences

(1) This section applies to offences under any of the following provisions of this Act, that is to say section 4(2) and (3), section 5(2) and (3), section 6(2) and section 9.

(2) Subject to subsection (3) below, in any proceedings for an offence to which this section applies it shall be a defence for the accused to prove that he neither knew of nor suspected nor had reason to suspect the existence of some fact alleged by the prosecution which it is necessary for the prosecution to prove if he is to be convicted of the offence charged.

(3) Where in any proceedings for an offence to which this section applies it is necessary, if the accused is to be convicted of the offence charged, for the prosecution to prove that some substance or product involved in the alleged offence was the controlled drug which the prosecution alleges it to have been, and it is proved that the substance or product in question was that controlled drug, the accused—

(a) shall not be acquitted of the offence charged by reason only of proving that he neither knew nor suspected nor had reason to suspect that the substance or product in question was the particular controlled drug alleged; but

(b) shall be acquitted thereof—
(i) if he proves that he neither believed nor suspected nor had reason to suspect that the substance or product in question was a controlled drug; or
(ii) if he proves that he believed the substance or product in question to be a controlled drug, or a controlled drug of a description, such that, if it had in fact been that controlled drug or a controlled drug of that description, he would not at the material time have been committing any offence to which this section applies.

(4) Nothing in this section shall prejudice any defence which it is open to a person charged with an offence to which this section applies to raise apart from this section.

* * *

Source 2

Psychoactive Substances Act 2016 ss 2–7

2 Meaning of 'psychoactive substance' etc

(1) In this Act 'psychoactive substance' means any substance which—
(a) is capable of producing a psychoactive effect in a person who consumes it, and
(b) is not an exempted substance (see section 3).

(2) For the purposes of this Act a substance produces a psychoactive effect in a person if, by stimulating or depressing the person's central nervous system, it affects the person's mental functioning or emotional state; and references to a substance's psychoactive effects are to be read accordingly.

(3) For the purposes of this Act a person consumes a substance if the person causes or allows the substance, or fumes given off by the substance, to enter the person's body in any way.

3 Exempted substances

(1) In this Act 'exempted substance' means a substance listed in Schedule 1.

(2) The Secretary of State may by regulations amend Schedule 1 in order to—
(a) add or vary any description of substance;
(b) remove any description of substance added under paragraph (a).

(3) Before making any regulations under this section the Secretary of State must consult—
(a) the Advisory Council on the Misuse of Drugs, and
(b) such other persons as the Secretary of State considers appropriate.

(4) The power to make regulations under this section is exercisable by statutory instrument.

(5) A statutory instrument containing regulations under this section may not be made unless a draft of the instrument has been laid before, and approved by a resolution of, each House of Parliament.

4 Producing a psychoactive substance

(1) A person commits an offence if—
(a) the person intentionally produces a psychoactive substance,
(b) the person knows or suspects that the substance is a psychoactive substance, and

(c) the person—
(i) intends to consume the psychoactive substance for its psychoactive effects, or
(ii) knows, or is reckless as to whether, the psychoactive substance is likely to be consumed by some other person for its psychoactive effects.
(2) This section is subject to section 11 (exceptions to offences).

5 Supplying, or offering to supply, a psychoactive substance

(1) A person commits an offence if—
(a) the person intentionally supplies a substance to another person,
(b) the substance is a psychoactive substance,
(c) the person knows or suspects, or ought to know or suspect, that the substance is a psychoactive substance, and
(d) the person knows, or is reckless as to whether, the psychoactive substance is likely to be consumed by the person to whom it is supplied, or by some other person, for its psychoactive effects.
(2) A person ('P') commits an offence if—
(a) P offers to supply a psychoactive substance to another person ('R'), and
(b) P knows or is reckless as to whether R, or some other person, would, if P supplied a substance to R in accordance with the offer, be likely to consume the substance for its psychoactive effects.
(3) For the purposes of subsection (2)(b), the reference to a substance's psychoactive effects includes a reference to the psychoactive effects which the substance would have if it were the substance which P had offered to supply to R.
(4) This section is subject to section 11 (exceptions to offences).

6 Aggravation of offence under section 5

(1) Subsections (2) to (10) apply if—
(a) a court in Scotland or Northern Ireland is considering the seriousness of an offence under section 5, and
(b) at the time the offence was committed the offender was aged 18 or over.
(2) If condition A, B or C is met the court—
(a) must treat the fact that the condition is met as an aggravating factor (that is to say, a factor that increases the seriousness of the offence), and
(b) must state in open court that the offence is so aggravated.
(3) Condition A is that the offence was committed on or in the vicinity of school premises at a relevant time.
(4) For the purposes of subsection (3) a 'relevant time' is—
(a) any time when the school premises are in use by persons under the age of 18;
(b) one hour before the start and one hour after the end of any such time.
(5) In this section—
- 'school premises' means land used for the purposes of a school, other than any land occupied solely as a dwelling by a person employed at the school;
- 'school' has the same meaning—

(a) in England and Wales, as in section 4 of the Education Act 1996;
(b) in Scotland, as in section 135(1) of the Education (Scotland) Act 1980;
(c) in Northern Ireland, as in Article 2(2) of the Education and Libraries (Northern Ireland) Order 1986 (S.I. 1986/594 (N.I. 3)).
(6) Condition B is that in connection with the commission of the offence the offender used a courier who, at the time the offence was committed, was under the age of 18.

(7) For the purposes of subsection (6) a person ('P') uses a courier in connection with an offence under section 5 if P causes or permits another person (the courier)—
(a) to deliver a substance to a third person, or
(b) to deliver a drug-related consideration to P or a third person.

(8) A drug-related consideration is a consideration of any description which—
(a) is obtained in connection with the supply of a psychoactive substance, or
(b) is intended to be used in connection with obtaining a psychoactive substance.

(9) Condition C is that the offence was committed in a custodial institution.

(10) In this section—
- 'custodial institution' means any of the following—
  (a) a prison;
  (b) a young offender institution, secure training centre, secure college, young offenders institution, young offenders centre, juvenile justice centre or remand centre;
  (c) a removal centre, a short-term holding facility or pre-departure accommodation;
  (d) service custody premises;
- 'removal centre', 'short-term holding facility' and 'pre-departure accommodation' have the meaning given by section 147 of the Immigration and Asylum Act 1999;
- 'service custody premises' has the meaning given by section 300(7) of the Armed Forces Act 2006.

(11) For the requirement for a court in England and Wales considering the seriousness of an offence under section 5 to treat certain matters as aggravating factors, see section 72 of the Sentencing Code.

7 Possession of psychoactive substance with intent to supply

(1) A person commits an offence if—
(a) the person is in possession of a psychoactive substance,
(b) the person knows or suspects that the substance is a psychoactive substance, and
(c) the person intends to supply the psychoactive substance to another person for its consumption, whether by any person to whom it is supplied or by some other person, for its psychoactive effects.

(2) This section is subject to section 11 (exceptions to offences).

* * *

Source 3

R v Lambert [2001] UKHL 37

3. The Court however certified three questions. The first in substance is whether it is an essential element of the offence of possession of a controlled drug under section 5 of the 1971 Act that the accused knew that he had a controlled drug in his possession; secondly whether in a charge contrary to section 5 the judge was right to direct the jury that the onus of proving the defence under section 28(2) imposed a legal rather than an evidential of burden of proof that the accused neither believed nor suspected nor had reason to suspect that the substance in question was a controlled drug. The third question asked whether the accused could, on an appeal after the Human Rights Act 1998 came into force, rely on an alleged breach of Convention rights by the investigating or prosecuting authority at a trial which took place before the Human Rights Act 1998 came into force.

4. On this appeal to your Lordships the appellant has contended that the direction by the judge, that the burden on the accused to establish the defence was a legal burden, violated Article 6 of the Convention rights set out in the Schedule to the 1998 Act. The essential preliminary question in the appeal, and it is an important question, is therefore whether an appellant can rely on the Act at a time when the Act is in force (i.e. after 2 October 2000) in respect of a prosecution and conviction at a date when the Act was not in force. In a sophisticated and forceful argument Mr Starmer has contended that he plainly can. He takes two different routes. The first is that section 6 of the 1998 Act provides '(1) . . . It is unlawful for a public authority to act in a way which is incompatible with a Convention right' (and by virtue of sub sections 6(3) and (4) 'public authority' includes a Court and the Judicial Committee of the House) unless by sub section (2) as the result of or in the case of 'one or more provisions of primary legislation, the authority could not have acted differently'.

. . .

16. The first question asks whether it is an essential element of the offence of possession of a controlled drug under section 5 of the Misuse of Drugs Act 1971 that the accused knows that he has a controlled drug in his possession. Bearing fully in mind the importance of the principle that the onus is on the prosecution to prove the elements of an offence and that the provisions of an Act which transfer or limit that burden of proof should be carefully scrutinised, it seems to me that the Court of Appeal in *R v McNamara* [1988] 87 Cr APP R 246 rightly identified the elements of the offence which the prosecution must prove. I refer in particular to the judgement of Lord Lane CJ at page 252. This means in a case like the present that the prosecution must prove that the accused had a bag with something in it in his custody or control; and that the something in the bag was a controlled drug. It is not necessary for the prosecution to prove that the accused knew that the thing was a controlled drug let alone a particular controlled drug. The defendant may then seek to establish one of the defences provided in section 5(4) or section 28 of the 1971 Act.

. . .

56. The Act also provides a person who is found to be in possession of a controlled drug with a number of defences. Section 5(4) contains a defence which is available in the case of a charge of simple possession under section 5(2) of the Act. It is a defence which proceeds on the assumption that the person knew or suspected that the thing which was in his possession was a controlled drug. Section 28 deals with the defences of lack of knowledge.
57. The Act does not contain a definition of 'possession', except that section 37(3) provides that for the purposes of the Act the things which a person has in his possession shall be taken to include anything subject to his control which is in the custody of another. But it is well settled that the expression embraces both a factual and a mental element. The factual element is that of control, as section 37(3) indicates. Unless the thing is in the person's control, albeit while it is in the custody of another, it cannot be said to be in his possession. The mental element is that of knowledge. It is the extent of the knowledge which has to be established that is in dispute in this case. This is the point raised by the first issue. The directions which were given to the jury by the trial judge were to the effect that, while it was necessary for the prosecution to prove that the person knew that the thing was in his control, it was not necessary for the prosecution to prove that he knew that the thing was a controlled drug.
58. I shall have to examine the provisions of the 1971 Act and the meaning of the word 'possession' further when I am dealing with the first and second issues. For the time being it is sufficient to notice that at the time of the trial the directions which were given to the jury by the trial judge were in accordance with the law

as it was understood to be at that time. According to this understanding, the mental element is satisfied if it is proved that the person knew that he had the thing in or subject to his control or, if it was in a container such as a bag, that it contained the thing which upon examination was found to be a controlled drug.

. . .

61. I would reject this argument. I consider the settled law to be correct on this point. As far as the Misuse of Drugs Act 1971 is concerned, there are two elements to possession. There is the physical element, and there is the mental element. The physical element involves proof that the thing is in the custody of the defendant or subject to his control. The mental element involves proof of knowledge that the thing exists and that it is in his possession. Proof of knowledge that the thing is an article of a particular kind, quality or description is not required. It is not necessary for the prosecution to prove that the defendant knew that the thing was a controlled drug which the law makes it an offence to possess. I observe that Mr Owen did not submit that it was necessary for the prosecution to prove that the defendant was aware that the thing was a class A, B or C drug, as the case may be, although the class into which the drug falls will usually be relevant to any sentence he may receive.

* * *

Source 4

R v Maginnis [1987] AC 303

The word 'supply,' in its ordinary natural meaning, conveys the idea of furnishing or providing to another something which is wanted or required in order to meet the wants or requirements of that other. It connotes more than the mere transfer of physical control of some chattel or object from one person to another. No one would ordinarily say that to hand over something to a mere custodier was to supply him with it. The additional concept is that of enabling the recipient to apply the thing handed over to purposes for which he desires or has a duty to apply it. In my opinion it is not a necessary element in the conception of C supply that the provision should be made out of the personal resources of the person who does the supplying.

. . .

LORD GOFF OF CHIEVELEY. My Lords, we are concerned in this case with the meaning of the word 'supply' as used in the expression 'with intent to supply it to another' in section 5(3) of the Misuse of Drugs Act 1971; though, since there is no reason to suppose that the word 'supply' in section 5(3) is intended to have any different meaning from the same word in section 4(1)(b) of the Act, which makes it unlawful 'to supply or offer to supply a controlled drug to another,' we are really concerned with the meaning of the word in both subsections.

The primary rule of construction is that we should attribute to words their natural and ordinary meaning, unless the context otherwise requires. So what is the natural and ordinary meaning of the word 'supply?' I hesitate to attempt a definition, especially as the word under consideration is not always very precisely used; but to me the word, as used in relation to goods, connotes the idea of making goods available to another from resources other than those of the recipient. This approach is, I consider, consistent with some of the dictionary meanings in the Shorter Oxford English Dictionary, for example, 'the act of making up a deficiency, or of fulfilling a want or demand,' and 'the act of supplying something needed.' It is also, I believe, consistent with the ordinary use of the word in everyday speech. So to deliver goods to a buyer or his agent under a contract of sale would obviously be to supply goods to that person, and indeed would perhaps provide the typical example of a supply of goods; though I can see no reason why the delivery of goods by way of gift should not also amount to a supply of goods.

But we are concerned in the present case with a deposit of goods; and I do not feel able to say that either the delivery of goods by a depositor to a depositee, or the redelivery of goods by a depositee to a depositor, can sensibly be described as an act of supplying goods to another. I certainly cannot conceive of myself using the word 'supply' in this context in ordinary speech. I ask myself: why should I not do so? I answer: I would not describe the delivery by the depositor to the depositee as a supply of goods, because the goods are not being made available to him but are rather being entrusted to him; and I would not describe the redelivery by the depositee to the depositor as a supply of goods, because the goods are simply being returned to him, rather than being made available to him from resources other than his own.

The context does not, as I see it, require any departure from the natural and ordinary meaning of the word. Moreover, the interpretation which I would give to the word, which I derive from my understanding of the use of the word 'supply' in ordinary speech, is consistent with the conclusion of the Court of Appeal in the present case. I must confess that, in a case where I am looking for the ordinary meaning of an ordinary word like 'supply,' I am much influenced by the fact that the three members of the Court of Appeal, having searched like myself for the ordinary meaning of the word, and having considered the earlier authorities, have reached the same conclusion as I myself have reached. In delivering the judgment of the court, Mann J. said [1986] Q.B. 618, 624:

> 'In ordinary language the cloakroom attendant, the left luggage officer, the warehouseman and the shoe mender do not "supply" to their customers the articles which those customers have left with them.'

* * *

Source 5

Sentencing Council Guideline: Possession of a controlled drug

Misuse of Drugs Act 1971, s 5(2)
Triable either way

Class A
Maximum: 7 years' custody
Offence range: Fine – 51 weeks' custody

Class B
Maximum: 5 years' custody
Maximum when tried summarily: 3 months' custody or level 4 fine
Offence range: Discharge – 26 weeks' custody

Class C
Maximum: 2 years' custody
Maximum when tried summarily: 3 months' custody or level 3 fine
Offence range: Discharge – Medium community order

. . .

Guideline users should be aware that the Equal Treatment Bench Book covers important aspects of fair treatment and disparity of outcomes for different groups in the criminal justice system. It provides guidance which sentencers are encouraged to take into account wherever applicable, to ensure that there is fairness for all involved in court proceedings.

Applicability

Step 1 – Determining the offence category

The court should identify the offence category based on the class of drug involved.

Category 1	Class A drug
Category 2	Class B drug
Category 3	Class C drug

Step 2 – Starting point and category range

Having determined the category at step one, the court should use the corresponding starting point to reach a sentence within the category range below. The starting point applies to all offenders irrespective of plea or previous convictions.

Offence category	Starting point (applicable to all offenders)	Category range (applicable to all offenders)
Category 1 (class A)	Band C fine	Band A fine – 51 weeks' custody
Category 2 (class B)	Band B fine	Discharge – 26 weeks' custody*
Category 3 (class C)	Band A fine	Discharge – Medium level community order*
* When heard summarily, the maximum penalty is 12 weeks' custody.		

...

Custodial sentences

Where the defendant is dependent on or has a propensity to misuse drugs and there is sufficient prospect of success, a community order with a drug rehabilitation requirement under part 10 of Schedule 9 of the Sentencing Code can be a proper alternative to a short or moderate length custodial sentence.

However, if a magistrates' court is of the opinion that the offending is so serious that the Crown Court should have the power to deal with the offender, the case should be committed to the Crown Court for sentence even if a community order may be the appropriate sentence (this will allow the Crown Court to deal with any breach of a community order if that is the sentence passed).

The table below contains a **non-exhaustive** list of additional factual elements providing the context of the offence and factors relating to the offender. Identify whether any combination of these, or other relevant factors, should result in an upward or downward adjustment from the starting point.

In particular, possession of drugs in prison is likely to result in an upward adjustment. In some cases, having considered these factors, it may be appropriate to move outside the identified category range.

Factors increasing seriousness
Statutory aggravating factors • Previous convictions, having regard to a) nature of the offence to which conviction relates and relevance to current offence; and b) time elapsed since conviction • Offence committed on bail **Other aggravating factors** • Possession of drug in prison • Presence of others, especially children and/or non-users • Possession of drug in a school or licensed premises • Large quantity* • Failure to comply with current court orders • Offence committed on licence • Attempts to conceal or dispose of evidence, where not charged separately • Established evidence of community impact

Factors reducing seriousness or reflecting personal mitigation
• No previous convictions or no relevant or recent convictions • Remorse • Positive character and/or exemplary conduct (regardless of previous convictions) • Small quantity* • Offender is using cannabis to help with a diagnosed medical condition • Determination and/or demonstration of steps having been taken to address addiction or offending behaviour • Serious medical conditions requiring urgent, intensive or long-term treatment • Isolated incident • Age and/or lack of maturity (which may be applicable to offenders aged 18–25) • Mental disorder or learning disability • Sole or primary carer for dependent relatives • Pregnancy, childbirth and post-natal care • Difficult and/or deprived background or personal circumstances • Prospects of or in work, training or education

*Whether a quantity is high or low will depend on the nature and potency of the drug.

Step 3 – Consider any factors which indicate a reduction, such as assistance to the prosecution

The court should take into account section 74 of the Sentencing Code (assistance by defendants: reduction or review of sentence) and any other rule of law by virtue of which an offender may receive a discounted sentence in consequence of assistance given (or offered) to the prosecutor or investigator.

. . .

Step 4 – Reduction for guilty pleas

The court should take account of any potential reduction for a guilty plea in accordance with section 73 of the Sentencing Code and the Reduction in Sentence for a Guilty Plea guideline.

Step 5 - Totality principle

If sentencing an offender for more than one offence, or where the offender is already serving a sentence, consider whether the total sentence is just and proportionate to the offending behaviour. See Totality guideline.

Step 6 - Ancillary orders

In all cases, the court should consider whether to make ancillary orders.
Forfeiture order - drug offences
Football banning order - on conviction
Ancillary orders - Magistrates' Court
Ancillary orders - Crown Court

Step 7 - Reasons

Section 52 of the Sentencing Code imposes a duty to give reasons for, and explain the effect of, the sentence.

Step 8 - Consideration for time spent on bail

The court must consider whether to give credit for time spent on bail in accordance with section 240A of the Criminal Justice Act 2003 and section 325 of the Sentencing Code.

* * *

Source 6

Sentencing Council Guideline: Supplying or offering to supply a controlled drug/Possession of a controlled drug with intent to supply it to another

Misuse of Drugs Act 1971 s 4(3), Misuse of Drugs Act 1971, s 5(3)
Supplying or offering to supply a controlled drug, Misuse of Drugs Act 1971 (section 4(3))
Possession of a controlled drug with intent to supply it to another, Misuse of Drugs Act 1971 (section 5(3))

Triable either way unless the defendant could receive the minimum sentence of seven years for a third drug trafficking offence under section 313 of the Sentencing Code in which case the offence is triable only on indictment.

Class A
Maximum: Life imprisonment
Offence range: High level community order - 16 years' custody

Class B
Maximum: 14 years' custody and/or unlimited fine
Offence range: Band B fine - 10 years' custody

Class C
Maximum: 14 years' custody and/or unlimited fine
Offence range: Band A – 8 years' custody

This offence is subject to statutory minimum sentencing provisions.

...

Step 1 – Determine the offence category

The court should determine the offender's culpability (role) and the harm caused (quantity) with reference to the tables below.

In assessing culpability, the sentencer should weigh up all the factors of the case to determine role. Where there are characteristics present which fall under different role categories, **or where the level of the offender's role is affected by the scale of the operation,** the court should balance these characteristics to reach a fair assessment of the offender's culpability.

Culpability demonstrated by the offender's role

One or more of these characteristics may demonstrate the offender's role. These lists are not exhaustive.

Leading role:

- Directing or organising buying and selling on a commercial scale
- Substantial links to, and influence on, others in a chain
- Close links to original source
- Expectation of substantial financial or other advantage
- Uses business as cover
- Abuses a position of trust or responsibility

Significant role:

- Operational or management function within a chain
- Involves others in the operation whether by pressure, influence, intimidation or reward
- Expectation of significant financial or other advantage (save where this advantage is limited to meeting the offender's own habit), whether or not operating alone
- Some awareness and understanding of scale of operation

Lesser role:

- Performs a limited function under direction
- Engaged by pressure, coercion, intimidation, grooming and/or control
- Involvement through naivety, immaturity or exploitation
- No influence on those above in a chain
- Very little, if any, awareness or understanding of the scale of operation
- Expectation of limited, if any, financial or other advantage (including meeting the offender's own habit)

Harm

In assessing harm, quantity is determined by the weight of the product. Where the offence is supply directly to users (including street dealing or supply in custodial institutions), the quantity of product is less indicative of the harm caused and therefore the starting point is not solely based on quantity. The court should consider all offences involving supplying directly to users as at least category 3 harm, and make an adjustment from the starting point within that category considering the quantity of drugs in the particular case.

Indicative quantities of the most common drugs (upon which the starting point is to be based) are given in the table below. Where a drug (such as fentanyl or its agonists) is not listed in the table below, sentencers should expect to be provided with expert evidence to assist in determining the potency of the particular drug and in equating the quantity in the case with the quantities set out in the guidelines in terms of the harm caused. There will often be no precise calculation possible, but courts are reminded that in cases of particularly potent drugs, even very small quantities may be held to be equivalent to large quantities of the drugs listed.

Category 1

- Heroin, cocaine – 5kg
- Ecstasy – 7,000 tablets*
- MDMA – 5kg
- LSD – 250,000 squares
- Amphetamine – 20kg
- Cannabis – 200kg
- Ketamine – 5kg
- Synthetic cannabinoid receptor agonists (for example 'spice') – very large quantity indicative of an industrial scale operation

Category 2

- Heroin, cocaine – 1kg
- Ecstasy – 1,300 tablets*
- MDMA – 1kg
- LSD – 25,000 squares
- Amphetamine – 4kg
- Cannabis – 40kg
- Ketamine – 1kg
- Synthetic cannabinoid receptor agonists (for example 'spice') – large quantity indicative of a commercial operation

Category 3

Selling directly to users
OR
Supply of drugs in a custodial institution
OR

- Heroin, cocaine – 150g
- Ecstasy – 200 tablets*
- MDMA – 150g
- LSD – 2,500 squares
- Amphetamine – 750g
- Cannabis – 6kg

- Ketamine - 150g
- Synthetic cannabinoid receptor agonists (for example 'spice') - smaller quantity between categories 2 and 4

Category 4

- Heroin, cocaine - 5g
- Ecstasy - 13 tablets*
- MDMA - 5g
- LSD - 170 squares
- Amphetamine - 20g
- Cannabis - 100g
- Ketamine - 5g
- Synthetic cannabinoid receptor agonists (for example 'spice') - very small quantity

Note - where the offence is selling directly to users or supply in a custodial institution the starting point is not based on quantity - go to category 3

*Ecstasy tablet quantities based on a typical quantity of 150mg MDMA per tablet.

Step 2 - Starting point and category range

Having determined the category at step one, the court should use the corresponding starting point to reach a sentence within the category range in the table below. The starting point applies to all offenders irrespective of plea or previous convictions.

An adjustment from the starting point, upwards or downwards, may be necessary to reflect particular features of culpability and/or harm (for example, the presence of multiple factors within one category, the presence of factors from more than one category (where not already taken into account at step 1), or where a case falls close to a borderline between categories).

Where the operation is on the most serious and commercial scale, involving a quantity of drugs significantly higher than category 1, sentences of 20 years and above may be appropriate, depending on the offender's role.

Sentencers should be aware that there is evidence of a disparity in sentence outcomes for this offence which indicates that a higher proportion of Black, Asian and Other ethnicity offenders receive an immediate custodial sentence than White offenders and that for Asian offenders custodial sentence lengths have on average been longer than for White offenders. There may be many reasons for these differences, but in order to apply the guidelines fairly sentencers may find useful information and guidance at Chapter 8 of the Equal Treatment Bench Book.

CLASS A	LEADING ROLE	SIGNIFICANT ROLE	LESSER ROLE
Category 1	**Starting point** 14 years' custody **Category range** 12–16 years' custody	**Starting point** 10 years' custody **Category range** 9–12 years' custody	**Starting point** 7 years' custody **Category range** 6–9 years' custody
Category 2	**Starting point** 11 years' custody **Category range** 9–13 years' custody	**Starting point** 8 years' custody **Category range** 6 years 6 months' - 10 years' custody	**Starting point** 5 years' custody **Category range** 3 years 6 months' - 7 years' custody

CLASS A	LEADING ROLE	SIGNIFICANT ROLE	LESSER ROLE
Category 3	**Starting point** 8 years 6 months' custody **Category range** 6 years 6 months' – 10 years' custody	**Starting point** 4 years 6 months' custody **Category range** 3 years 6 months' – 7 years' custody	**Starting point** 3 years' custody **Category range** 2–4 years 6 months' custody
Category 4	**Starting point** 5 years 6 months' custody **Category range** 4 years 6 months' – 7 years 6 months' custody	**Starting point** 3 years 6 months' custody **Category range** 2–5 years' custody	**Starting point** 18 months' custody **Category range** High level community order – 3 years' custody

CLASS B	LEADING ROLE	SIGNIFICANT ROLE	LESSER ROLE
Category 1	**Starting point** 8 years' custody **Category range** 7–10 years' custody	**Starting point** 5 years 6 months' custody **Category range** 5–7 years' custody	**Starting point** 3 years' custody **Category range** 2 years 6 months' – 5 years' custody
Category 2	**Starting point** 6 years' custody **Category range** 4 years 6 months' – 8 years' custody	**Starting point** 4 years' custody **Category range** 2 years 6 months' – 5 years' custody	**Starting point** 1 year's custody **Category range** 26 weeks' – 3 years' custody
Category 3	**Starting point** 4 years' custody **Category range** 2 years 6 months' – 5 years' custody	**Starting point** 1 year's custody **Category range** 26 weeks' – 3 years' custody	**Starting point** High level community order **Category range** Low level community order – 26 weeks' custody
Category 4	**Starting point** 18 months' custody **Category range** 26 weeks' – 3 years' custody	**Starting point** High level community order **Category range** Medium level community order – 26 weeks' custody	**Starting point** Low level community order **Category range** Band B fine – Medium level community order

CLASS C	LEADING ROLE	SIGNIFICANT ROLE	LESSER ROLE
Category 1	**Starting point** 5 years' custody **Category range** 4–8 years' custody	**Starting point** 3 years' custody **Category range** 2–5 years' custody	**Starting point** 18 months' custody **Category range** 1–3 years' custody
Category 2	**Starting point** 3 years 6 months' custody **Category range** 2–5 years' custody	**Starting point** 18 months' custody **Category range** 1–3 years' custody	**Starting point** 26 weeks' custody **Category range** 12 weeks' – 18 months' custody

CLASS C	LEADING ROLE	SIGNIFICANT ROLE	LESSER ROLE
Category 3	**Starting point** 18 months' custody **Category range** 1–3 years' custody	**Starting point** 26 weeks' custody **Category range** 12 weeks' – 18 months' custody	**Starting point** High level community order **Category range** Low level community order – 12 weeks' custody
Category 4	**Starting point** 26 weeks' custody **Category range** High level community order – 18 months' custody	**Starting point** High level community order **Category range** Low level community order – 12 weeks' custody	**Starting point** Low level community order **Category range** Band A fine – Medium level community order

Factors increasing seriousness

Statutory aggravating factors:

- Previous convictions, having regard to a) nature of the offence to which conviction relates and relevance to current offence; and b) time elapsed since conviction
- Offender used or permitted a person under 18 to deliver a controlled drug to a third person
- Offender 18 or over supplies or offers to supply a drug on, or in the vicinity of, school premises either when school in use as such or at a time between one hour before and one hour after they are to be used.
- Offence committed on bail

Other aggravating factors include:

- Exploitation of children and/or vulnerable persons to assist in drug-related activity
- Offender supplies or offers to supply a drug to a person under the age of 18
- Exercising control over the home of another person for drug-related activity
- Targeting of any premises where children or other vulnerable persons are likely to be present
- Exposure of drug user to the risk of serious harm over and above that expected by the user, for example, through the method of production or subsequent adulteration of the drug
- Exposure of those involved in drug dealing to the risk of serious harm, for example through method of transporting drugs
- Exposure of third parties to the risk of serious harm, for example, through the location of the drug-related activity
- Attempts to conceal or dispose of evidence, where not charged separately
- Presence of others, especially children and/or non-users
- Presence of weapons, where not charged separately
- Use of violence (where not charged as separate offence or taken into account at step one)
- Failure to comply with current court orders
- Offending took place in prison (unless already taken into consideration at step 1)
- Offender was supplying or involved in the supply of drugs into prison

- Offence committed on licence or post sentence supervision
- Established evidence of community impact
- Use of sophisticated methods or technologies in order to avoid or impede detection

Factors reducing seriousness or reflecting personal mitigation

- Involvement due to pressure, intimidation or coercion falling short of duress, except where already taken into account at step one.
- Supply only of drug to which offender addicted
- Mistaken belief of the offender regarding the type of drug, taking into account the reasonableness of such belief in all the circumstances
- Isolated incident
- No previous convictions or no relevant or recent convictions
- Remorse
- Positive character and/or exemplary conduct (regardless of previous convictions)
- Determination and/or demonstration of steps having been taken to address addiction or offending behaviour
- Serious medical conditions requiring urgent, intensive or long-term treatment
- Age and/or lack of maturity (which may be applicable to offenders aged 18–25)
- Mental disorder or learning disability
- Sole or primary carer for dependent relatives
- Pregnancy, childbirth and post-natal care
- Offender's vulnerability was exploited
- Difficult and/or deprived background or personal circumstances
- Prospects of or in work, training or education

* * *

■ YOUR TURN

Have a go at answering question 2, remembering the guidance on page 22.

- Refer to the structured approach in the SRA's assessment criteria on page 23.
- Conduct focused legal research of the question given using case law, legislation and texts.
- When assessing whether or not a source is relevant, ask yourself: does it deal with the same type of offence as the question? Does it interpret a provision of the Act that you are dealing with? Is it found on the same or similar facts, and is that authority binding?
- List all relevant issues which you will discuss and any issues that arise.
- Provide a concise and well-reasoned analysis based on your research, avoiding too much jargon and complexity.
- Timings are important: you will need to prepare and write your answer in 60 minutes. Before tackling this question, work out how much time you will allocate to reading the sources, planning your response and then writing and reviewing your answer.

SQE1 Functioning legal knowledge link

As highlighted in chapter 1 of ***Revise SQE: Criminal Practice***, understanding procedures such as arrest powers, custody rules and the role of evidence is vital. When faced with unfamiliar offences in SQE2 legal research, a firm understanding of these frameworks may help you to evaluate statutory provisions more confidently.

EVALUATING YOUR ANSWER

When you have attempted question 2, mark it yourself against the SQE2 legal research assessment criteria. Do you think your attempt met the threshold standard?

Now compare your attempt with the following key legal points and two sample answers to the question. A circled number indicates that commentary is provided for this part of the answer. The commentary explains whether or not the sample answer satisfies the assessment criteria and is likely to meet the SQE2 threshold standard.

➥Key legal points: question 2

In this assessment, part or all of the following sources are relevant to the question:

- Misuse of Drugs Act 1971 ss 4, 5, 28
- *R v Lambert* [2001] UKHL 37
- *R v Maginnis* [1987] AC 303
- Sentencing Council Guidelines: Supplying or offering to supply a controlled drug/ Possession of a controlled drug with intent to supply it to another

The following sources are not relevant to the question:

- Psychoactive Substances Act 2016 ss 2–7
- Sentencing Council Guidelines: Possession of a controlled drug

Key legal points include the following:

- The key offence here is possession with intent to supply a Class A drug, contrary to s 5(3) of the Misuse of Drugs Act 1971. Section 4 makes it an offence to supply or offer to supply a controlled drug and s 5 covers the intent to supply.
- *R v Maginnis* is relevant as it is a leading case in the interpretation of the meaning of 'supply' under the Act. This case held that returning drugs to their owner can constitute supply if it enables further use or distribution. *R v Lambert* addresses the burden of proof under s 28 of the Misuse of Drugs Act, which clarifies that the defendant only needs to raise an evidential burden when claiming a lack of knowledge of the drug.
- The sources that are identified above as being irrelevant are such because the Psychoactive Substances Act 2016 applies only if the substance is not already controlled by the Misuse of Drugs Act. For this question, the issue is with cocaine rather than a 'legal high' drug. The Sentencing Council guidelines for possession of a controlled drug are irrelevant because they are for simple possession rather than with an intent to supply. These are two different offences.
- For the offence to be made out, the prosecution must prove two elements: (1) the possession of the controlled drug and (2) the intent to supply it to another person:
  1. As to the possession, this can be actual possession of the drug (where it is found on the defendant's person) or constructive possession (whereby the defendant has knowledge and control over the drug even if not physically in their possession). With this scenario, you should consider whether Sarah's presence in the room provides sufficient evidence for possession of the drugs; was she close enough to the drugs to imply knowledge and control?

2. The intent to supply is usually inferred from evidence. This can include a large quantity of the drug, drug paraphernalia such as snap bags or weighing scales, quantities of cash, or communications or text messages that suggest distribution.

- A key legal point in relation to the issue of 'holding' the drugs for someone else is that the defendant may still be guilty of possession with intent to supply even if they did not intend to distribute the drugs themselves. This is further confirmed by *R v Maginnis*, whereby 'supply' can amount to returning drugs to another person. You should consider whether Sarah's account that she did not know about the existence of the drugs and that she had no intention of handling them could rebut the inference that she was acting as a custodian. Is there enough evidence to infer intent to supply?
- If convicted of any offence, sentencing is assessed by the Sentencing Council's guidelines. In this case the relevant guidelines are those for drug offences. There are two key factors which make up the guidelines - culpability and harm:
  - Culpability is the role that the defendant played in the offending behaviour, that is, how blameworthy they are. Did they play a lead role, or a lesser role but still involved?
  - Harm is the scale and consequences of the offence. For drugs cases this is usually measured on the quantity and type of drug and its impact on others, including the risk posed.
- Sentencing is like a sliding scale that can go up or down depending on the defendant and the offending behaviour. This is assessed using mitigating and aggravating factors. Mitigating factors are those that work in the defendant's favour, while aggravating factors are those that do not.
  - Sarah's mitigating factors could be that she has no prior convictions; her previous caution was minor and from three years ago; she is still relatively young (her caution was from when she was 19 so we can infer that she is now 22 as three years have passed); and she may have played a lesser role or was naive in her role. Each of these factors will be considerations when advising on the sentence which may be imposed if she is convicted.
  - The aggravating factors in the case may be the drugs that were recovered in a space where Sarah was, the presence of cash and packaging materials in close proximity and the potential exposure to others as a result of the drugs.
- The range for a lesser role in the offending with a significant quantity of the drug could be between three and seven years' custody. Remember from your criminal practice functioning legal knowledge that a guilty plea could lead to a reduction in the sentence that is imposed.

SAMPLE ANSWER 1 TO QUESTION 2

I have reviewed the details of Sarah Smith's case regarding the imminent charge under s 5(3) of the Misuse of Drugs Act 1971 for possession with intent to supply Class A drugs. In short, I do not consider the evidential basis for conviction to be strong without further supporting material. However, if she is convicted, a custodial sentence is highly likely. I will go through my findings below. ❶

Relevant law ❷

Section 5(3) of the Misuse of Drugs Act 1971 states that 'it is an offence for a person to have a controlled drug in his possession, whether lawfully or not, with intent to supply it to another in contravention of section 4(1) of this Act'. The prosecution must prove both possession and intent to supply beyond a reasonable doubt. ❸

Possession

Sarah was found inside a property where cocaine, cash and snap bags were recovered. The drugs were on a coffee table near her and the other individuals who were in the property with her. She states that she was visiting to play video games and denies any knowledge of the drugs. No drugs were found on her person.

For possession to be made out, Sarah must be shown to have knowledge of the drugs and a degree of control over them, as held in *R v Lambert* [2001] UKHL 37. This case further stipulates that mere presence near drugs is not sufficient to amount to possession, stating at paragraph 57 that, 'unless the thing is in the person's control, albeit while it is in the custody of another, it cannot be said to be in his possession'. Without forensic evidence such as an admission or CCTV, constructive possession may be difficult to prove. ❹

It is relevant to note that, even if Sarah were 'holding' the drugs for another person, this would still constitute possession for the purpose of s 5, provided that she had knowledge of the drugs and the ability to exercise control over them albeit temporarily. The defence could not rely solely on the drugs belonging to someone else.

Based on the current information, it is unlikely that Sarah's presence alone demonstrates possession. However, the proximity will result in a natural inference being drawn and she might be expected to explain certain things such as how long she was there, whether she saw any drugs, evidence of a video console in the property and evidence of her playing any games. ❺

Intent to supply

Intent to supply is usually inferred from contextual evidence such as the quantity of the drugs, packaging and large amounts of cash. *R v Maginnis* [1987] AC 303 clarifies that supply includes any form of transfer, even without profit. However, it also requires the inference of intent based on reliable indicators.

While the scene suggests a drug supply environment, there is no direct link between Sarah and the items found (there was no cash or paraphernalia on her person). Unless further evidence arises - such as cell site evidence, DNA on packaging or telephone evidence - intent to supply may not be proven against Sarah individually. ❻

Sentencing

If Sarah is convicted, sentencing will follow the Sentencing Council Guidelines for possession of a controlled drug with intent to supply it to another, and is done in two stages. Culpability assesses how blameworthy the offender is, and it is determined by their role, intent and level of involvement in the offence. In Sarah's case, if she was only present and unaware of the drugs and there is no evidence of her handling or distributing them, she may be assessed as having a lesser role. However, if she is convicted at trial this will be on the Crown's full case. The benefit of an early plea is that she can enter a basis of such, which could indicate a lesser role if there is evidence of it.

The assessment of harm is based on the type and quantity of the drug involved. For Class A drugs, as in this case, there are four categories. The information I have been given indicates that there was a large quantity of drugs but the exact weight is unknown. If it exceeds 1kg then it may fall into category 2 harm even if Sarah's role was minimal.

The court may adjust the sentence based on aggravating and mitigating factors, and apply a reduction for an early guilty plea up to one-third if Sarah decides to plead guilty. ❼

Aggravating and mitigating factors

Some aggravating factors could be: drugs found in the residential area, Sarah's proximity to packaging and cash, and the potential exposure to other people.

Some mitigating factors could be: Sarah's lack of previous convictions, her possible naivety and limited role in the offending behaviour, and a lack of evidence of financial gain or active supply. ❽

Conclusion

In summary, based on the current information that I have, the charge of possession with intent to supply may be difficult to prove without direct evidence of control or involvement. However, if convicted, Sarah is likely to receive a custodial sentence, depending on role and drug quantity.

I would advise gathering all the evidential material including forensic reports and witness testimony.

Please let me know if I can assist further with this matter. ❾

COMMENTARY

❶ This headnote paragraph directs the assessor to the candidate's answer immediately, which is recommended in the SQE2 assessment and also in practice. A partner will often need to access a Day One Solicitor's findings without having to sift through a lengthy text, so a clear statement of the candidate's decision helps to establish a conclusion before delving into the given reasoning. Foreshadowing the conclusion also demonstrates the candidate's structured approach to their research and provides a straightforward response to the partner's question.

❷ A structured analysis with subheadings reflects strong communication skills, which are critical in the profession. Adding headings also shows that the candidate understands the key components of the question and the points from the research that the answer needs to address. Remember that your response should be client-focused in order to meet the assessment criteria.

❸ The candidate quotes from the statute correctly and provides a definition of the offence in a succinct and straightforward way, which reveals their understanding. Importantly, this also demonstrates the candidate's ability to translate complex language into layperson's terms, so that the partner will be able to use this definition when explaining the legal situation to Sarah. This approach addresses the requirement of the assessment criteria to use clear, concise, precise and acceptable language.

❹ By exploring the specific behaviours from the scenario, the candidate demonstrates an awareness of the constituent parts of the relevant offence that they have gleaned from the research sources. They can therefore apply the law correctly as required by the assessment criteria. The candidate also cites authorities appropriately: *R v Lambert* is correctly referenced to support the discussion on possession and the need for knowledge and control.

❺ This is a balanced analysis of the facts and their likely impact for the client, which helpfully anticipates the prosecution's arguments.

❻ The candidate shows that they can differentiate primary and secondary issues, exercising their discretion and judgement to come to a clear conclusion. *R v Maginnis* is cited correctly to expand the definition of supply and emphasise the requirements. This shows competence in locating and applying the precedents given.

7 The section on sentencing draws from the correct Sentencing Council guidelines, clearly explaining culpability, harm and the role-based classification. The candidate assesses harm based on drug quantity and identifies the likelihood of a category 2 harm level. They also correctly mention the possibility of sentence reduction if Sarah pleads guilty, which demonstrates an understanding of procedure in criminal litigation.

8 The answer lists both aggravating and mitigating factors, which are important parts of the sentencing procedure. The clear and logical approach to Sarah's situation demonstrates a sound understanding of the case at hand and her position; the candidate is focused on the client and is able to apply the law correctly.

9 The conclusion offers a reasoned summary of the legal position and practical guidance on the next steps, including gathering evidence to assist the case. This reflects the candidate's ability to deliver professional and client-focused advice as required by the assessment criteria.

Does this answer meet the threshold?

This sample answer is likely to meet the assessment threshold. The candidate has identified and used relevant source material, and referenced specific parts of the sources that clearly communicate the law that applies to the issues being discussed. The conclusion directly addresses the key points (whether an offence has been committed) that the partner will be considering at this stage of the litigation. The candidate reaches this conclusion after a straightforward but thorough explanation of how the law applies to the facts in the case. The answer discloses no critical misunderstandings.

The response uses formal language throughout and maintains a clear structure. Each section flows logically and headings clarify the subject matter. This meets the SQE2 criteria for presenting advice in a structured and accessible format.

Now consider the second sample answer to question 2.

■ SAMPLE ANSWER 2 TO QUESTION 2

Following my review of Sarah Smith's case and her potential charges, I provide the following analysis. 1

Relevant law

Section 2 of the Psychoactive Substances Act 2016 prohibits possession with intent to supply psychoactive substances. Under this framework, action may be taken if the substances involved are capable of affecting a person's mental state. Given that cocaine was recovered in the property and that it can impact cognition and an individual's behaviour, this Act may be applicable. 2

Furthermore, the Misuse of Drugs Act 1971 governs offences involving controlled drugs, such as cocaine. Its relevance may be limited depending on whether the charge relates to general possession or psychoactive intent.

General drug principles should be considered because Sarah was found in a property where cocaine, snap bags and cash were located on a table near her. Although no drugs were on her person, there is a question about whether she had personal possession or involvement in supplying substances.

Possession

Under the Sentencing Council Guidelines for possession of a controlled drug, custody is not automatic and there are alternative disposals depending on the class of the drug recovered. Cocaine is Class A but the guideline suggests that lower-level possession may be treated with community orders or fines. Since Sarah did not have the drugs on her, the possession element may be weak, and she might be found not guilty of the offence. ❸

Even if Sarah was holding the drugs for someone else, it should still count as possession because the law is focused on whether she knew about the drugs and whether she could control them, not whether she owned them. ❹

Intent to supply

The guideline for possession sentencing also explains that the context of a situation matters. Sarah denied knowledge and did not have packaging on her personally. This means the intent to supply may be minimal. If this cannot be shown, it would be more appropriate to treat this as a lower-level possession offence. There is the possibility that she was unaware and had no plan to distribute any drugs. ❺

Sentencing

If Sarah is convicted, then the sentencing guidelines for possession offences will apply. Since she has no previous convictions and was not carrying drugs herself, the starting point could be a fine or conditional discharge. She may not meet the custody threshold, particularly with mitigating factors such as no intent and limited awareness. ❻

Conclusion

It is likely that the Psychoactive Substances Act 2016 is relevant here, particularly due to the comment made by the police officer about her looking 'very disturbed', which indicates a lack of cognitive understanding and mental functioning. ❼

I recommend gathering more information to assess the seriousness of the potential offending, but I do not think that custody would be appropriate if Sarah is convicted. ❽

COMMENTARY

❶ There is an attempt at an introduction here, but it falls short of the foreshadowing as demonstrated in sample answer 1 and does not add much value to the answer. A well-structured answer would provide a concise overview of the legal principles and a summary of the analysis and/or outcome, in this case whether or not Sarah's action meets the threshold for a s 5(3) offence.

❷ This summary is not accurate for the offence with which Sarah is potentially being charged. Setting out that the Psychoactive Substances Act 2016 is relevant here demonstrates a misunderstanding of the situation and the sources that have been provided. The SQE2 assessment will test your ability to apply the law to a real-life scenario in order to resolve a given issue, and you need to show detailed analysis and application of your findings to the facts, to ensure that the legal frameworks are understood by the partner/assessor and the correct advice given to them.

❸ This candidate makes the mistake of assuming that some of the sources are relevant to the research question when they are not. Remember that irrelevant sources will be provided in the assessment to test your ability to determine the correct law for that scenario. You should base your answer on the sources provided, but supported by your previous knowledge, judgement and intuition rather than assumptions or panic-stricken logic.

4 These paragraphs set out the correct principles for an offence of possession of a controlled drug – but the case that the candidate is being asked to deal with is a potential possession with intent to supply; unfortunately, the analysis is therefore incorrect for this scenario. In the assessment, make sure that you read the question and sources carefully and thoroughly, so that you can give a full and appropriate answer.

5 This section confuses intent to supply with possession-based sentencing outcomes. There is no reference to supporting case law such as *R v Maginnis* and there is no engagement with evidential factors which are given in the scenario such as packaging or the drug quantity. The analysis is speculative and lacks authority, failing to meet the criteria for a well-reasoned response.

6 Sentencing is dealt with using the wrong guidelines. The candidate claims that Sarah may receive a fine or conditional discharge if convicted – this advice could be detrimental to a client who is being charged with a much more severe offence of possession with intent to supply Class A drugs, where a custodial sentence is far more likely. The candidate does not mention culpability or harm, nor do they mention the different sentencing ranges that would have been more suitable here. This answer therefore fails to apply the law correctly as required by the assessment criteria.

7 This is the first mention of the comment made by the police officer and should not be in the conclusion. A conclusion should summarise the findings and provide recommendations on next steps or the current position, rather than include new information. It is crucial that the conclusions in your research responses are explicitly based on the sources provided which are relevant to the research question. This is the crux of the research assessment, and by failing to mention the source(s) that supports these statements the candidate fails to meet the first assessment criterion: identify and use relevant sources and facts. Remember that some sources are designed to test your decision-making and intellectual legal skills rather than guide your answer.

8 As a more general point, declarative statements are rarely helpful, unless preceded by clear information and rationale; here the statement was not proceeded by such supportive material. When utilising a declarative statement in response to a research question, always ask yourself 'why?'. You will force yourself to add value to your research responses.

Does this answer meet the threshold?

This answer is not likely to meet the SQE2 threshold criteria, even though it uses broadly the same format as answer 1. The key is how the author's research skills are demonstrated. The candidate has not demonstrated that they can identify and use relevant sources and information, and they have based their advice on some sources that are irrelevant to the situation at hand and the alleged offences. The answer falls short because it does not clearly apply the law or guidelines to Sarah's specific situation; instead, it summarises the sources without showing how the facts affect the likelihood of a possession with intent to supply charge or potential sentencing. Legal reasoning and use of the sources are missing and therefore the assessment criteria are not met.

■ KEY POINT CHECKLIST

This chapter has covered the following key knowledge points:

- The SQE2 assessment criteria for legal research and how to apply them in the context of criminal litigation.
- A suggested structure for approaching an SQE2 legal research question in criminal litigation.
- Examples of legal research responses that are either likely or unlikely to meet the threshold standard, with full commentary on their strengths and weaknesses.

■ SUMMARY AND REFLECTION

Although this is an obvious point, the starting point for the SQE2 legal research assessment is always the question set in the email from the partner. Your response and advice must be tailored to the question; this is not a general discussion or an academic essay. In practice, you would be providing information for a busy professional, and it might help you to keep this thought in your mind throughout the assessment. A clear and concise writing style makes it easier for the audience to understand and interpret what they are reading, which is why this is required by the assessment criteria. Think about how you would digest the information presented in your answer: if it is muddled to you as the author, it will probably be muddled for the reader/assessor.

Make sure you have evidenced your use of the sources provided, so long as they are relevant to the question asked. The best way to do this is to refer directly to the sources in your answer and quote from them if you can. But be careful not to just replicate a source as the answer: you must *use* the sources, not merely *adopt* them.

Structure is your friend: the more structured your answer, the better your research will appear. Much like a maths question, good legal research answers show their working out.

3

Legal writing

■ MAKE SURE YOU KNOW

This chapter deals with the skill of legal writing in the context of criminal litigation. This is one of the legal skills that will be assessed on day one of the SQE2 assessments in either criminal litigation or dispute resolution (see the Introduction for more detail). It is important for you to remember that the SQE2 can test candidates' knowledge not only of the processes associated with criminal litigation but also the application of general criminal law and evidence principles to those processes. It is therefore essential that you read this revision guide once you are familiar with the contents of ***Revise SQE: Criminal Law*** and ***Revise SQE: Criminal Practice***. When attempting these practice questions, you will need to build on your knowledge from the SQE1 course and apply your learning to the requirements of the SQE2 assessments.

This chapter provides examples of how different options for criminal litigation, evidence and practice could arise in the context of a legal writing SQE2 assessment.

■ SQE ASSESSMENT ADVICE

As you work through this chapter, remember to pay particular attention in your revision to:

- the inclusion of relevant facts in the sample answers
- the way in which letters and emails are structured, and how this could be applied generally
- the ways in which the advice given in the sample answers is tailored to the client/recipient and the information the candidate was given about them
- how the sample answers use clear and concise language
- how the law is applied to the client's situation
- the way in which any ethical or professional conduct issues are identified and resolved.

See the Appendix for the SRA's performance indicators in legal writing and how to demonstrate your competency in this skill.

■ INTRODUCTION TO LEGAL WRITING IN CRIMINAL LITIGATION

It is likely that your SQE2 assessment will replicate scenarios that occur in day-to-day legal practice. As with all disciplines, a key aspect of practising in the field of criminal litigation is the ability to follow advice given by a solicitor to a client with a clearly articulated written communication. Your SQE2 assessment in legal writing is a computer-based assessment, in which a memo or email from a partner asks you to provide advice to a client to follow up on a previous conversation or enquiry from the client. Whilst the question itself will give you some direction about the areas you need to cover in your letter or email, you will be required to apply your functioning legal knowledge of those areas to the scenario and communicate the relevant advice to the client clearly and concisely in writing. This chapter will provide examples of how you can do this and meet the assessment criteria for SQE2 legal writing at the same time.

Your response to the SQE2 legal writing assessment will be more successful if you approach the question in a structured manner. Try adopting the following method:

1. Once you have read the question, note down what exactly the client would like advice on.
2. Note down the key legal and procedural points that you feel need to be communicated to the client.
3. You can then sketch a plan for your response, using headings to structure the letter or email around those key legal and procedural points.
4. Write your answer.
5. Review your answer, keeping in mind the SQE2 legal writing assessment criteria.

Assessment technique

When reviewing your answer, read the sentences aloud in your head. This technique stops you from skipping words and enables you to check for spelling error and typos more easily. Another commonly taught technique is to read sentences backwards, as this usually allows you to spot errors in your writing with ease.

SQE2 legal writing assessment criteria

Try to remember these points as you construct your answer, and refer back to them as you review our sample answers in this chapter:

Skills

1. Include relevant facts.
2. Use a logical structure.
3. Advice/content is client- and recipient-focused.
4. Use clear, precise, concise and acceptable language which is appropriate to the recipient.

Application of law

5. Apply the law correctly to the client's situation.
6. Apply the law comprehensively to the client's situation.
7. Identify any ethical and professional conduct issues and exercise judgement to resolve them honestly and with integrity.

For further support and guidance on how to meet the SQE2 legal writing assessment criteria, see ***Introduction to Written Legal Skills for SQE2***, chapter 3, Legal writing.

In chapter 6 of ***Revise SQE: Criminal Practice***, we covered visual identification evidence and *Turnbull* guidance. Question 1 below demonstrates how your knowledge of this topic could be tested in the context and format of an SQE2 legal writing assessment.

■ QUESTION 1

Email to candidate

From: Partner
Sent: 20 November 202#
To: Candidate
Subject: Rex v Jordan Smith

This morning one of our caseworkers saw a new client, Jordan Smith, and I have been asked to look at this case. This client faces one count of attempted murder. The Crown's case is as follows:

The injured party (IP) is Arthur Terry (age 69). He was walking home from the HSBC bank after drawing out some money from a cash machine to place in his grandson's birthday card. The IP seems to have challenged a group of men, telling them that he 'didn't fight in a war for them to doss about, drinking and smoking all day long, taking benefits'. He was then attacked by two of the men, pushed to the ground and kicked repeatedly. The attack caused the IP to suffer four broken ribs, significant bruising and, most notably, a fractured skull, as a result of a kick to the head. The IP remains as an inpatient in hospital but is no longer in intensive care.

Police officers came upon the attack whilst attending to obtain a witness statement from the bank manager regarding another unconnected matter. They intervened: one of the attackers got away, but after an elongated foot chase where the pursuing officer did not have a constant view of the suspect, and in the context where the observation of the attack was only 'fleeting', our client was arrested. The police officer alleges our client was the other attacker as they were running away from the scene and wearing the same football shirt as the person being chased (see the police officer's witness statement in Attachment 1).

On arrest, our client had in their possession two small plastic bags containing what is thought to be cannabis, together with £100 in cash and a mobile phone. In interview, our client denied the attack, and said they ran because they don't like the police. In conference with our caseworker, our client denies being the other attacker. They say that they were wearing that particular football shirt as there was a football match earlier that afternoon, which they had watched in a pub. They now say that they ran from police as they were dealing drugs and didn't want to get caught.

Our client has significant experience of the criminal justice system; they have 15 convictions for 28 offences, mostly related to drugs. They are concerned about the officer's identification and thinks they have 'just nicked me for it as I was there, and they needed to arrest someone for it'. The client has also asked if they should just plead guilty to get it over with, as they rather enjoyed being in prison last time.

Please write a letter to Jordan in my name, explaining the following:

1. **The strength of the prosecution's case.**
2. **Any potential issues with the identification evidence from the officer.**
3. **Your advice on plea.**

This client knows their way around the courts and studied a basic introduction to law during their last period in custody, so please give simple legal explanations where you can, to satisfy them.

Our client is: Jordan Smith, 56 Long Street, Newcastle NE30 9DZ.

Thanks,

Partner

Attachment:
Witness statement of PC Jamie Reynolds

Note to candidates:
Please assume that all issues in relation to client care/money laundering have already been dealt with by the partner. You do not need to make enquiries about the client's source of funds.

Attachment 1

STATEMENT OF WITNESS
(Criminal Procedure Rules, r 16.2; Criminal Justice Act 1967, s 9)

Name: PC 8421 Jamie Reynolds
Age: Over 18

This statement, signed by me, is true to the best of my knowledge and belief and I make it knowing that if it is tendered in evidence I shall be liable to prosecution if I have wilfully stated in it anything which I know to be false or do not believe to be true.

I am PC 8421 Jamie Reynolds. I am a police constable based in Lancashire Police.

I observed a physical altercation outside the HSBC bank whilst on a visit for a different, unrelated matter. A man was on the ground being kicked by two individuals. I intervened and the attackers fled the scene.

I gave chase to one of the individuals but lost sight periodically due to pedestrian traffic. Eventually I apprehended a man, JAMIE SMITH, who was wearing a red and white football shirt, consistent with one of the attackers who I had seen.

Upon arrest, he was in possession of two small bags containing a substance believed to be cannabis, a mobile phone and £100 in cash. Mr SMITH denied involvement in an attack, stating that he ran as he dislikes the police.

Signed: *PC Jamie Reynolds*
Date: 25 October 202#

* * *

■ YOUR TURN

Have a go at answering question 1, remembering the guidance on page 70.

- Refer to the structured approach in the SRA's assessment criteria on page 71.
- Create a list of the most salient legal points raised by the question.
- Timings are important: you will need to prepare and write your answer in 30 minutes.

SQE1 Functioning legal knowledge link

When approaching this question, consider your learning from SQE1 on inchoate offences such as attempted murder, explained in ***Revise SQE: Criminal Law***, chapter 3. You should also consider how best to advise clients about courtroom procedure and making a plea; see ***Revise SQE: Criminal Practice***, chapter 4, to refresh your knowledge.

EVALUATING YOUR ANSWER

When you have attempted question 1, mark it yourself against the SQE2 legal writing assessment criteria. Do you think your attempt met the threshold standard?

Now compare your attempt with the following key legal points and two sample answers to question 1. A circled number indicates that commentary is provided for this part of the answer. The commentary explains whether or not the sample answer satisfies the assessment criteria and is likely to meet the SQE2 threshold standard.

➥Key legal points: question 1

- Explore potential issues relating to the identification evidence, as the whole case relies on the eyewitness testimony of one pursuing officer. For example, consider:
  - the length of time the suspect was under observation
  - the varying distances involved in an elongated foot chase
  - the environment (officer running, carrying equipment, stress of the chase, etc)
  - the time and circumstances between the original observation and the arrest.
- Consider the *Turnbull* guidelines on dealing with eyewitness identification evidence, which are applicable in this case.
- The defendant should plead not guilty as he does not accept the Crown's case. Pleas should never be entered on the basis of commercial reality, especially in offences as serious as this.
- There is a potential sentence of life imprisonment. If convicted even with credit, the sentence will be measured in years rather than months.
- Remember that citations are not appropriate to include in your answer letter to the client.

■ SAMPLE ANSWER 1 TO QUESTION 1

[*The law firm's address and contact details*]

Mx Jordan Smith
56 Long Street
Newcastle
NE30 9DZ
20 November 202#

Dear Mx Smith, ❶

Re: Ongoing criminal proceedings: Attempted murder

Thank you for consulting our firm in relation to the charges you presently face. I am sorry we met under such circumstances, but we are thankful for your trust, nonetheless.

The purpose of this letter is to provide advice on the two principal questions that you asked our caseworker in your conference this morning. These two issues are:

1. The evidence of the police officer identifying you as the suspect; and
2. Whether you should enter a guilty plea to the offence. ❷

The identification evidence ❸

The disclosure from the Crown Prosecution Service states that you were arrested following an elongated police foot chase when the arresting officer made a 'fleeting' observation of a man who attacked the injured party (Mr Terry). When a court assesses the reliability of identification from a witness, it is guided by a number of principles. Having regard to those principles, I form the view that the police identification evidence could not be described as strong or compelling. ❹

A number of factors lead me to this conclusion:

1. The officer's initial observation is described as 'fleeting'; this word itself is discussed heavily in relevant cases. Fleeting glances are accepted to be generally unreliable.
2. The fact that the officer lost sight of the suspect he was chasing for some time also makes the evidence more difficult for the prosecution in your case. There is every chance the officer could have taken a wrong turn, started following a different person, and so on.
3. Finally, in respect of the distinctive football shirt that the Crown alleges the suspect was wearing, which they say matches the shirt you were wearing on arrest: again, whilst the evidence here does help the Crown, it is capable of being undermined. Given your instructions it is likely that many people were wearing the same shirt because of the football match that took place on that day. ❺

As for the issue of you running from the scene, it is your view that it can be easily explained - you initially told police that you ran because you do not like dealing with the police. You now have a different explanation, which you feel can be easily justified. Advancing that explanation will result in exposing your drug offending, but in the context of a charge as serious as attempted murder you may wish to give thought to doing so. Your involvement in drug dealing could be treated as a separate matter, although it will not detract from the explanation for why you left the scene. It is important to consider carefully whether you wish to provide alternative accounts as they could raise questions as to your credibility.

An application to dismiss can be made to the court in advance of any trial, on account of the unreliable nature of the Crown's principal witness, the police officer. On the current case the trial judge would likely warn the jury in relation to your proper concerns as to the reliability of the identification evidence. ❻

Your plea

I understand from my colleague that you were considering pleading guilty to 'get it over with' as you have quite enjoyed being in prison. I can only advise you against that course of action in the strongest possible terms. In the account you provided to my colleague, you do not accept the offence as alleged and you tell us that you were not the attacker. I cannot advise you to plead guilty to an offence that you do not accept committing. This is not a question of convenience and should not be treated as such. Although I accept that you are not repulsed by the prospect of a custodial sentence, I must caution you that the maximum sentence of an offence of attempted murder is life imprisonment. This is an order that will have an impact on the rest of your life and is not something to be trivialised. Furthermore, should you plead guilty, I would be limited as to the mitigation that I can provide the court as it would be taken that you are accepting the Crown's case in full by that plea. My advice, based on your instructions to us, is that you should plead not guilty. ❼

I will write again in due course, once we receive an update as to this matter, including any new information or decisions regarding the case. I will also correspond with the local bar to find an appropriate barrister to instruct on your behalf. We will take no further positive or binding action without consulting you. ❽

Yours sincerely,

Partner

COMMENTARY

❶ Note the use of the prefix Mx: as you are not advised how this client identifies, this is the safest course of action and accords with the general principles of equality and diversity. Once pronouns are known, they should be adopted.

❷ As with any legal writing (letter) exercise, the first section appropriately outlines the purpose of the letter. The candidate allows the partner to introduce themselves, then helpfully uses a numbered list for the key points. This allows the lay client to understand the letter's themes before delving into its contents.

❸ The use of subheadings allows the client to manoeuvre through the letter easily. This is helpful to clients who may find complex concepts of law difficult to understand, especially if they interrelate to one another.

❹ The candidate puts forward their conclusion firmly, and then backs it up with reasoning. This demonstrates a correct application of the law, as required by the assessment criteria, and is expressed in precise and clear language.

❺ Note how the letter refers to the material gained from the conference with the caseworker (as is often the case in criminal proceedings). This shows the assessor that the candidate is making use of the information provided by the client, and will likely meet the assessment criteria by providing client-focused advice. The letter also demonstrates the candidate's understanding of the law and responds to the partner's instructions regarding the client's legal knowledge. The candidate compartmentalises the issues where the officer's evidence falls short of reliability by making direct links to the circumstances of this client's case.

❻ The candidate presents a balanced view of the likely outcome of the client revealing his possession of drugs to be the real reason he ran away, allowing the client to decide on their course of action. This demonstrates a client-focused response as required by the assessment criteria. The candidate also correctly acknowledges the court's procedural safeguards – the judge's likely warning to the jury in relation to the reliability of identification evidence and the impact of the Crown's main witness being deemed unreliable.

❼ In the section headed 'Your plea', the advice is robust and firm, as it needs to be, and meets the assessment criteria by explaining the lay client's position in language that they will understand. This letter is not an answer to an academic essay but a piece of written work focused on providing succinct and relevant advice to the client. The section directly links back again to the information received from the client in conference and refers to relevant facts. It does not rehearse matters unnecessary to the advice and does not recount, for example, that the client denies intention to kill, because such a denial is included in the denial of the attack. The advice given by the candidate discharges their ethical obligations relating to the advice on plea, again satisfying the assessment criteria.

❽ The final paragraph is a useful device to demonstrate the candidate's familiarisation with the workings of criminal practice, and supports the assessor's overall impression of their competency.

Does this answer meet the threshold?

This sample answer contains the relevant information that the candidate is asked to provide, and is likely to meet the threshold standard for SQE2 legal writing. The facts outlined in the response are clearly set out and relevant to the question, and the candidate has homed in on the important details. The structure is logical in its approach and would help the client reader in following the information that is being communicated. The content of the letter is focused on the recipient to an appropriate level and uses plain English that the client would be able to understand.

As far as the law is concerned, the application is accurate and directly relevant to the client's situation. The law is applied comprehensively and no ethical guidelines are breached in relation to the advice given. It is clear that the candidate has exercised their own considered judgement in drafting this letter. Note that each of the assessment criteria for legal writing are dealt with and, where appropriate, the assessor is directed specifically to the areas of the letter which deal with those criteria.

Now consider the second sample answer to question 1.

■ SAMPLE ANSWER 2 TO QUESTION 1

[*The law firm's address and contact details*]

Mr Smith ❶
56 Long Street
Newcastle
NE30 9DZ
20 November 202#

Dear Mr Smith

Your criminal charge(s)

This is an advice letter, please read it carefully. ❷

You don't admit being the attacker therefore you are not guilty of your charge, as you have not committed an act more than merely preparatory to the commission of a relevant offence. You should therefore plead not guilty to the charge of attempted murder. You did not intend to kill the IP. ❸

You say that you want to plead guilty to get it over with. I can understand this position - and frankly, given your record of offending, this will not make a significant difference to your position as far as your character goes. You might wish to take the inevitable custodial sentence for this matter in order to resolve the matter without the inconvenience of a trial, and of course you would get credit for doing so. ❹

We could also speak to the CPS and see if they can offer you a s 18 GBH charge, or even a s 20. This may well lead to a suspended sentence in any event and would certainly be a good result for you in the circumstances. ❺

As far as the ID evidence goes, I agree with you - the police probably did just arrest you because you vaguely fit the bill and were running away. The fact you were dealing drugs doesn't concern us, I will not advise you in relation to what you do about that. Only the attempted murder. ❻

The ID evidence is weak, and we'll probably be able to get this case thrown out at a fairly early opportunity. ❼

Leave it with me. ❽

Sincerely,

Partner

COMMENTARY

❶ Addressing the letter to 'Mr Smith' and not including the client's first name, Jordan, creates the risk that an unintended person could open the letter, such as Jordan's father, brother or son. This is imprecise language, and as such does not meet the assessment criteria requirements.

❷ This letter opens poorly: the subject line is vague and the specific charge is not mentioned until the end of the second paragraph. Note also that the candidate uses a run-on sentence (here, and in other places in the letter), which is grammatically incorrect: the comma after 'letter' should be a semi-colon, or a full stop with the next phrase as a new, complete sentence. When you review your answer, look out for mistakes like this as they indicate a casual approach to writing and could create a poor impression on your assessor.

❸ The letter then deals with the client's questions out of order and for no apparent reason. When structuring your response, try to adopt the partner's/client's order unless you can see a reason for not doing so.

This paragraph does not consider the main defence point in context: it does not place the advice on the foundations of a proper analysis of the facts as required by the assessment criteria but rather on a two-line summary of the position. The letter then notes that the client 'did not intend to kill the IP'. There are two weaknesses here: (1) the point on intent, whilst true, is not the basis upon which the client defends, so is not appropriately included; (2) the language and tone are inappropriate for a client letter. For example, the abbreviation 'IP' (injured party) is industry vernacular that is not readily understood by lay clients; the candidate uses the legal term 'merely preparatory' without proper expansion of what this means for the client; finally, the candidate includes a contraction in their writing ('don't' instead of 'do not'), which is too informal for professional communications with a client. On the whole, this paragraph has not been drafted with the recipient (client) in mind and as such would not meet the assessment criteria.

❹ The passage frames a guilty plea as a pragmatic decision to avoid the delays of trial rather than as an admission of moral or legal weight. It suggests that, given the individual's previous record, the plea will have limited impact on character assessment and presents acceptance of a custodial sentence as a practical means of resolving the matter more efficiently. From a professional standpoint, it demonstrates clarity but comes across as unduly pragmatic, informal and not focused on the impact of the guilty plea on the client's life.

❺ Whilst communication with the CPS such as this can be appropriate, it is not so in these circumstances. Neither s 18 nor s 20 offences could be accepted by the client on their current instructions. The client denies the offence and the plea therefore should be one of not guilty: this is the only advice that should be given. The candidate is not applying the law correctly to the client's situation and fails to meet the assessment criteria here.

❻ This is superficial and casual advice. Simply agreeing with the client without analysing the reliability or legal significance of the identification evidence is a weak approach and fails to demonstrate professional competence in addressing such a critical issue in the case.

7. Here the candidate provides the prospect of a successful application to dismiss. However, this is unprofessional as a client should never be given unsubstantiated hope in relation to potential applications, and certainly not in this manner. Applications to dismiss fail more than they succeed, so any suggestion of such an application succeeding should be properly considered, ideally by a higher courts advocate or counsel with experience of such applications, before it is given.
8. No information is given on the next steps. The vague 'Leave it with me' line is a poor attempt at a conclusion.

Does this answer meet the threshold?

The second answer likely falls short of the threshold standard. Although the content of the advice is largely correct, the manner in which the letter has been written does not demonstrate the candidate's competencies adequately.

The facts outlined in the response are not clearly set out, and there is some focus on irrelevant facts for this question. The structure is not logical in its approach, and it is unclear whether the structure of this response helps the reader follow the information being communicated. The content of the letter is not focused on the recipient to an appropriate level; it does not use plain English and could be difficult for the client recipient to read and understand. As far as the law is concerned, the application is not clear or accurate, and it does not apply directly to the client's situation. The law is not applied comprehensively, and ethical guidelines are breached in relation to the advice given.

As you know, SQE2 can assess any of the areas in the SQE1 criminal practice specification. Question 2 shows how another part of the specification may appear in the legal writing assessment for SQE2: the allocation of a case. This task also demonstrates how you might need to address procedural issues in your assessment.

■ QUESTION 2

Email to candidate

From: Partner
Sent: 24 June 202#
To: Candidate
Subject: Rex v Janey Simons

I have been asked to review the case of a client who is facing a charge of theft under £200 and is due to appear at the magistrates' court later this month for their first hearing. This matter has come to my attention after one of our caseworkers met the client this morning.

The client, Ms Janey Simons, is concerned that the magistrates who will hear her case might be too 'case-hardened' and might not believe her version of events. She knows a few of the magistrates personally and is under the impression that any trial she faces in the magistrates' court will be unfair, with the bench possibly biased against her. She has expressed a strong preference for being tried by a jury and has asked if it is possible to request a trial by jury instead. She would feel more comfortable being tried by members of the public rather than by a panel of magistrates or even a district judge, but would like to have more information about the trial process before making a decision.

The offence in question appears relatively straightforward in terms of the facts. The prosecution alleges that Ms Simons stole a handbag from beneath a table in a train station. The handbag contained valuable items, including a mobile phone, a tablet, some cash and a purse with credit cards. The alleged theft occurred while the handbag's owner went to the lavatory. The client believed she would have the owner's consent to appropriate the property to enable her to hand it in to the police. Ms Simons is particularly anxious about the potential consequences of a criminal conviction, as she is hoping to pursue a career in nursing. She has no previous criminal convictions.

Unfortunately, I have been called to deal with another urgent matter, so I need you to write a letter to Ms Simons for me which addresses the following:

1. **Your advice regarding the allocation of her case - provide a clear explanation of whether the case is likely to be heard in the magistrates' court or if there is any possibility of requesting a trial by jury in the Crown Court.**
2. **A brief explanation of the trial process as it applies to her case for both courts, particularly in terms of her options for trial allocation.**

Please ensure that your response explains the legal processes in a clear and understandable manner.

Client details: Janey Simons, 151 Oak Road, Bristol BS41 3PQ.

Best regards,

Partner

* * *

■ YOUR TURN

Have a go at answering question 2, remembering the guidance on page 70.

- Refer to the structured approach in the SRA's assessment criteria on page 71.
- Create a list of the most salient legal points raised by the question.
- Timings are important: you will need to prepare and write your answer in 30 minutes.

SQE1 Functioning legal knowledge link
You are reminded to consider chapter 7 of ***Revise SQE: Criminal Law***, which outlines the relevant point of theft offences, including the key elements set out in s 1 of the Theft Act 1968 and further detailed in ss 2–6. See also chapter 4 of ***Revise SQE: Criminal Practice***, which covers the legal principles and procedures surrounding allocation of a case and how a court or defendant chooses whether their case should be tried summarily or on indictment.

EVALUATING YOUR ANSWER

When you have attempted question 2, mark it yourself against the SQE2 legal writing assessment criteria. Do you think your attempt met the threshold standard?

Now compare your attempt with the following key legal points and two sample answers to question 2. A circled number indicates that commentary is provided for this part of the answer. The commentary explains whether or not the sample answer satisfies the assessment criteria and is likely to meet the SQE2 threshold standard.

➥Key legal points: question 2

- Identify theft as an offence that is triable either way.
- Identify that the magistrates' court is likely to retain jurisdiction, given this is a simple fact pattern and does not present any complex legal questions.
- Discuss the allocation procedure.
- Discuss the concept of election.
- Explore potential issues in relation to the allocation, and discuss the merits and pitfalls of the two possibilities:
  - a summary trial (in the magistrates' court) or
  - a trial on indictment (before a judge and jury in the Crown Court).
- Provide clear and focused advice in relation to the two issues raised to the caseworker.

■ SAMPLE ANSWER 1 TO QUESTION 2

[*The law firm's address and contact details*]

Ms Janey Simons
151 Oak Road
Bristol
BS41 3PQ
24 June 202#

Dear Ms Simons

Your pending charge of theft

Thank you for consulting this firm in relation to the charges you presently face.

The purpose of this letter is to provide advice on the two principal questions that you asked our caseworker today, namely issues in relation to whether you can be tried by a jury, and what the process of trial involves. This letter is written on the basis, as we understand, that you will be pleading not guilty at your first hearing. ❶

Trial by jury, or trial in the magistrates' court ❷

Theft, with which you are charged, is an offence that could be tried in the magistrates' court or Crown Court. The principles of allocation will determine where your trial takes place:

1. The first step is for the magistrates to consider whether they are capable of hearing your trial. This will depend on how complicated the case might be and whether there are any novel issues of law. In your case there are no complicating factors or complex issues of law, and it is likely that the magistrates' court will say that they can hear your trial.
2. At this point, you can choose whether to accept a trial in the magistrates' court or to request for your trial to be heard by a judge and jury at the Crown Court. We would make these representations on your behalf but it is a choice only you can make, and there are differences between the two. Statistically you are more likely to be found not guilty in the Crown Court. Some people say that this is because magistrates are more prosecution-minded, although I cannot say if that is the right reason. However, you should also consider that trials in the magistrates' court often take place relatively quickly, and are more informal than their Crown Court alternative.

The decision on allocation is an important one, and you are not expected to make it based on this letter alone. You will have further advice prior to the allocation hearing, which you should wait for before making any firm decision. ❸

Trial process

The trial process does not differ substantially between a trial in the magistrates' court and in the Crown Court. As a result, you can take my commentary below to be in respect of both venues.

The first substantive step in a trial is the opening speech from the prosecution lawyer, who will outline what the case is about. The prosecution has to prove the case, so they are setting out what they will seek to prove. In your type of case, there would be no opening speech from your defence advocate.

The prosecution will then call their evidence. In your case, they are likely to call the police officers who arrested you, and they may call a train station employee in relation to any CCTV evidence. When the prosecutor asks questions of the witnesses, this is called 'examination in chief'. Witnesses are presented in turn: each witness is subject to examination in chief and then questions are asked by your lawyer in your defence, which is called 'cross-examination'. When the prosecution has called all of their witnesses, they will close their case. This is the halfway point of the trial.

The defence lawyer now presents the defence. You are not obliged to give evidence in your own defence but not doing so would mean that the magistrates or jury are open to make inferences from your decision. In your case it is likely that you would give evidence in your own defence. You too would be subject to examination in chief by your lawyer, and then cross-examination by the prosecutor.

If you choose to call witnesses in your defence, they would appear after you. You may wish to think about whether anyone could help your defence or highlight your good character, considering that you have no previous convictions.

When all witnesses have given evidence, both the prosecutor and your lawyer will make a closing speech, either to the magistrates' court bench or to a jury if the trial is held in the Crown Court. After the speeches you will await your verdict, of guilty or not guilty. ❹

I hope this has been of assistance and that we will discuss the trial process as we progress through the case. I will write again in due course to advise you in terms of the logistics for your upcoming hearing later this month. It is likely that you will be represented by a solicitor from this firm, unless it becomes more appropriate to instruct a barrister (a specialist advocate). We will take no further positive or binding action without consulting you. ❺

Yours sincerely,

Partner

COMMENTARY

❶ This is a strong opening to the letter: the candidate politely thanks the client for approaching them, outlines the purpose of the letter and the two issues to be addressed, and clearly states the client's basis of plea. When you prepare for your legal writing assessment, you might find it useful to formulate a similar template for the beginning of your letter or email, to help your writing flow. This opening shows that the candidate is using the relevant information from the instructions and will be focusing on the client's concerns, as required by the assessment criteria.

❷ Headings are used correctly in this letter. This demonstrates logical structure and directly shows the assessor that the candidate is meeting the assessment criteria.

❸ The explanation demonstrates a clear, client-focused approach by presenting the options in a balanced and accessible manner. The information is structured logically, explaining allocation and then the client's options, and is written in plain English, not legal jargon. Highlighting both practical and statistical considerations such as likelihood of acquittal demonstrates competence, as it allows the client to make their own informed decision.

❹ This is a clear description of the trial process that will be easy for the client to follow. By linking the procedural stages to the client's case in terms of witnesses, evidence and the significance of prior convictions, the client can understand better what to expect from a trial. This section also ensures the client grasps the process without feeling overwhelmed, fulfilling the criteria for clarity, client focus and practical application. The candidate demonstrates their understanding of the legal system and responds to the partner's' instructions in an appropriate order: the letter compartmentalises the client's concerns in a way that is both logical and appropriately structured.

❺ This paragraph outlines the likely representation arrangements and next steps in the process in clear language. The statement that no action will be taken without the client's consent prioritises the client's best interests. No reference is made to matters irrelevant to the client's best interests, such as fees recoverable by solicitors. This is evidence of sound, ethical and rational judgement and meets the assessment criteria.

Does this answer meet the threshold?

The sample answer above contains the relevant information that the candidate is asked to provide, including an explanation of the charge and the court and an outline of the trial process. It demonstrates clear communication, identification of key legal issues and a good understanding of procedure that would make a client feel at ease. It is likely to meet the threshold standard for SQE2 legal writing as it satisfies the assessment criteria, despite not covering every possible point and making some minor stylistic and procedural errors (for example, at times commentary is rather informal and speculative in relation to the magistrates' court, and the candidate could adopt a more professional tone here).

Now consider the second sample answer to question 2.

■ SAMPLE ANSWER 2 TO QUESTION 2

[*The law firm's address and contact details*]

Simons
151 Oak Road
Bristol
BS41 3PQ
24 June 202#

Dear Janey ❶

Your commission of theft ❷

Thank you for consulting this firm in relation to your charge.

This is a simple case with no issues of law, so the magistrates' court will likely accept jurisdiction. You could elect a trial before a Judge and Jury in the Crown Court; however, you will be waiting a very long time for that. The magistrates' court is quicker, and I assume you'll just want to get this over with. ❸

As far as the trial process is concerned - it will be different in the magistrates' court or the Crown Court.

In the Crown Court a jury would be sworn in in accordance with the Criminal Procedure Rules, and then the Crown would present its opening statement outlining what you have done and why that is an offence. Then the police will give their evidence, which you can challenge in cross-examination. After that, you can give evidence, but you don't have to if you don't want to. You can call other witnesses if you wish.

Then the prosecution lawyer, and your barrister, will give their closing submissions summarising the evidence and legal arguments. The jury will retire to deliberate and return a verdict of guilty or not guilty in respect of each charge. ❹

If you are convicted, there is a chance you could go to prison, but you probably won't. ❺

I'll see you at your hearing later this month. Give me a shout if you don't have the dates. ❻

Sincerely,

Partner

COMMENTARY

❶ This letter is too informal for a piece of legal writing and is also much too brief. A letter to a client should be professional and follow a formal structure; the tone of this letter is inappropriate, as though the candidate were writing to a friend. Remember to use language that is clear, precise, concise and appropriate, in order to meet the assessment criteria.

The candidate displays a slipshod attitude in addressing the client at the beginning of the letter: the client's title has been missed in the address, and in the salutation only her first name has been used. Using the client's prefix and surname is a more suitable salutation: 'Dear Ms Simons'.

❷ This letter opens poorly: the subject line itself suggests the client is guilty. Be very mindful of inappropriately including your own assumptions when you phrase the subject line.

❸ The letter then considers the first question raised, as to allocation. This is a rushed piece of writing, and the candidate does not adequately consider the points that will most significantly influence the client's decision on election. The response shows a lack of client focus, as the instructions have clearly stated that the most important thing to the client is to avoid a conviction rather than have a quick decision.

❹ This is a brief and incomplete explanation of the trial process that will not assist the client in deciding on the place of trial. Although the candidate says that the process is different, they only describe the process in the Crown Court. Their response also uses legal terminology, which may not be easily comprehensible to a nervous and inexperienced client. This is a prime example of where using plain English is necessary for letter writing and communicating with the client; the candidate has not met the assessment criteria here, and this explanation will only serve to confuse the client further and enhance their worry.

❺ The candidate discusses sentencing at this point, although this was not part of the instructions in the partner's email. Remember to keep the focus of the question in your mind when you write your response, so that you only address the tasks given to you. The candidate's approach of jumping straight to the prospect of custody is also highly inappropriate and demonstrates a lack of focus on the client's requirements.

6 The sign-off is informal ('Give me a shout' is inappropriate for a professional letter) and does not reflect the solemnity of the client's situation. Furthermore, if dates are known they should be included, or the candidate should confirm that they will inform the client once dates are available.

Does this answer meet the threshold?

The second letter likely falls short of the SQE2 threshold standard. Although the content of the advice is largely correct, the manner in which the letter has been written does not demonstrate the SRA's stipulated competencies adequately and the candidate fails to meet the assessment criteria. In particular, the letter adopts a casual and dismissive tone that is inappropriate for communication to a client. The response could be improved by explaining the client's circumstances in detail and addressing outcomes rather than being speculative.

KEY POINT CHECKLIST

This chapter has covered the following key knowledge points:

- The SQE2 assessment criteria for legal writing and applying them in the context of criminal litigation.
- A suggested structure for approaching an SQE2 legal writing question in criminal litigation.
- Examples of written answers that are either likely or unlikely to meet the threshold standard, with full commentary on their strengths and weaknesses.

SUMMARY AND REFLECTION

At the beginning of your SQE2 legal writing assessment, take a few minutes to ensure that you understand the question properly and can think holistically about different aspects of your response such as structure, the characteristics of your audience and how to apply the law to the client's scenario. Draw up a plan for your letter before you start writing, and make sure that your response meets the SQE2 assessment criteria for legal writing.

Remember that you are being assessed on how you communicate the correct and relevant law in the context of your client's scenario - it is so important to remember that SQE2 are skills assessments. You have proven your knowledge in SQE1; here you use that knowledge to prove your skills.

Practice makes perfect, and writing will come more naturally to you the more you do it. Take every opportunity to practise writing clear, well-structured letters, and remember to make the language appropriate to your audience. Use plain, jargon-free English when writing to clients, but when writing to the other side's solicitors you will need to use the correct legal terminology.

Now take the time to reflect and consider what you might still need to work on, and whether you feel completely confident in your legal writing skills in the context of criminal litigation.

4

Legal drafting

■ MAKE SURE YOU KNOW

Legal drafting is an important skill that any lawyer in practice must acquire. It is one of the legal skills assessed on day one in either criminal litigation or dispute resolution (see the Introduction for more detail). The SQE2 assessment will require candidates to produce a clear, precise and professionally structured legal document that reflects their understanding of criminal litigation processes. Many documents follow the same or very similar style, structure and format, and as a result you can often adopt the same 'formula' when approaching the task of drafting a legal document. In this chapter, we shall use the production of defence statements and skeleton arguments to demonstrate this point. You may find it useful to refer to chapter 5 of ***Revise SQE: Criminal Practice*** before attempting the questions in this chapter as it will refresh your learning on case management.

When preparing for the SQE2 legal drafting assessment for criminal litigation, we recommend that you practise structuring legal arguments concisely. Make sure that you deal clearly with:

- the charges faced by the defendant
- the evidence being relied upon
- any procedural aspects that crop up.

■ SQE ASSESSMENT ADVICE

As you work through this chapter, remember to pay particular attention in your revision to:

- using clear, precise, concise and acceptable language that is appropriate for the target audience of the intended document
- including relevant facts in the sample answers
- structuring the documents appropriately, adding headings and subheadings and adopting logical formatting
- complying with precedents, language and formatting (where appropriate)
- checking your work for clarity and accuracy in the content (ie the law) and how it is written (ie grammar and spelling)
- adapting any precedent or draft document provided to fit the context of the instructions and the client's needs
- identifying ethical or professional conduct issues in the task.

See the Appendix for the SRA's performance indicators in legal drafting and how to demonstrate your competency in this skill.

■ INTRODUCTION TO LEGAL DRAFTING IN CRIMINAL LITIGATION

For the legal drafting assessment, you will be expected to draft a legal document or parts of a legal document for a client. This may require you to draft a document from a precedent provided, amend a document that has already been drafted or draft a document from scratch.

The assessment is designed to reflect a real-life task that a solicitor may be given. Effective drafting is essential in the legal process: you must demonstrate an ability to identify facts, apply appropriate law/statutory provisions, communicate complex legal concepts to clients and other parties precisely and professionally, and express legal arguments in a logical, structured and persuasive manner. The draft should comply with rules and advance the client's position to the court. Drafted documents must be clear, accurate, concise and tailored to the reader, which could be a lay client, the court or the opposing party.

Attention to detail, use of plain English and maintaining professionalism are critical for any legal drafting exercise. It is also vital to maintain ethical standards, including acting in the best interest of the client in the administration of justice. You must be alert to recognising ethical issues and confident in resolving them honestly and with integrity.

The key to success in your SQE2 legal drafting assessment is approaching the question in a structured manner. Try adopting the following method:

1. Identify what you are being asked to draft.
2. Identify the key issues raised in the instructions or supporting materials (ie what is the client seeking?)
3. Use the materials provided and your own knowledge to locate the relevant legislation, case law (if applicable) or precedent.
4. Ensure your drafting is accurate and appropriately structured for the reader.
5. Tailor your drafting of the document to the needs of the client - use clear language and appropriate formalities.
6. Review your answer for spelling and grammatical errors, keeping in mind the assessment criteria.

Assessment technique

A common problem that arises in the SQE2 legal drafting assessment is lack of precision in presenting the required information. It is important to adopt a carefully considered and structured approach to drafting: ensure that your draft documents are accurate and clear so that a lay reader, in this case the assessor, can quickly and easily identify your legal reasoning.

SQE2 legal drafting assessment criteria

Try to remember these points as you construct your answer, and refer back to them as you review our sample answers in this chapter:

Skills

1. Use clear, precise, concise and acceptable language.
2. Structure the document appropriately and logically.

Application of law

3. Draft a document which is legally correct.
4. Draft a document which is legally comprehensive.
5. Identify any ethical and professional conduct issues and exercise judgement to resolve them honestly and with integrity.

For further support and guidance on how to meet the SQE2 legal drafting assessment criteria, see ***Introduction to Written Legal Skills for SQE2***, chapter 4, Legal drafting.

In chapter 6 of ***Revise SQE: Criminal Law***, we considered the core principles of non-fatal offences against the person. Question 1 below demonstrates how your knowledge of this topic could be tested in the context and format of an SQE2 legal drafting assessment.

■ QUESTION 1

Email to candidate

From: Partner
Sent: 10 October 202#
To: Candidate
Subject: Mrs Sarah Walker - defence statement required

We are instructed by Mrs Sarah Walker, who has been charged with an offence of assault occasioning actual bodily harm (ABH), contrary to s 47 Offences Against the Person Act 1861.

The allegation relates to an incident at a children's playground in Nottingham on 24 July 202#. The complainant, Mrs Amanda Doyle, claims that Mrs Walker pushed her with force and without provocation, causing her to fall and sustain minor facial bruising along with a brief period of concussion.

Mrs Walker denies the allegation. She states that she was acting in self-defence. Mrs Walker says that she was at the playground with her child and that Mrs Doyle approached her in an aggressive manner. Mrs Walker claims that Mrs Doyle was verbally abusive, shouting and screaming at her, and then grabbed her arm and got close to her face during the confrontation. In response, Mrs Walker claims that she pushed Mrs Doyle away instinctively as she thought she was about to be assaulted and did not want to be hurt.

There were multiple witnesses to the incident, but their accounts differ:

- Some witnesses are uncertain, suggesting that Mrs Doyle might have been the aggressor and Mrs Walker might have been acting in self-defence.
- Others support the prosecution's version, indicating that Mrs Walker acted without provocation and used an excessive level of force.

Mrs Walker has been provided with initial prosecution disclosure and has pleaded not guilty. The matter is listed for trial at Nottingham Magistrates' Court in a few months. Whilst we are not required to serve a defence statement, Mrs Walker has specifically instructed us to do so.

Attached to this email are a proof of evidence of Mrs Walker (Attachment 1) and two witness statements (Attachments 2 and 3). I would like you to draft a defence statement for Mrs Walker that is suitable for service, using the defence statement template (Attachment 4).

The defence statement should set out the following:

1. The nature of Mrs Walker's defence, including any particular defences on which she will rely.
2. The matters of fact that Mrs Walker takes issue with, and the reasons why.
3. The particulars of the matters of fact on which Mrs Walker intends to rely for the purposes of the defence.

4. Points of law that we wish to make, including points about admissibility of evidence or abuse of process, and any authority relied on.
5. Whether we are going to rely on an alibi (ie an assertion that Mrs Walker was in a place, at a time, inconsistent with her having committed the offence), particulars including:
   a. the name, address and date of birth of any witness who Mrs Walker believes can give evidence in support of that alibi, or
   b. if those details are not available, any information that might help identify or find that witness.

Please also include in the defence statement any requests for disclosure, the prosecution witnesses required for trial and any defence witnesses that will be called to give evidence.

Many thanks,

Partner

Attachments:

1. Proof of evidence of Mrs Sarah Walker
2. Witness statement of Paige Farmer
3. Witness statement of Henry Harden
4. Defence statement template

Attachment 1

PROOF OF EVIDENCE OF MRS SARAH WALKER

SARAH WALKER will say:

1. I live at 24 Sunnyhill Lane, Nottingham. I am 34 years of age and intend to plead NOT GUILTY to the charge of assault occasioning actual bodily harm.
2. On 24/07/202#, I was at the children's playground in Nottingham with my young child. I was supervising him and had not been involved in any argument or confrontation before the incident occurred.
3. At around 3.15 P.M., the complainant, Mrs Amanda Doyle, approached me in what I felt was an aggressive and confrontational manner. She was shouting loudly and appeared very angry. I did not know why she was directing this at me.
4. Mrs Doyle was very close to me, and she was raising her voice, swearing and pointing. She continued to shout in front of both of our children, which made me feel threatened and embarrassed.
5. During this, Mrs Doyle grabbed hold of my left arm. I thought she was going to assault me further. I felt genuinely frightened and believed that I was about to be seriously hurt.
6. As a result, I instinctively pushed her away. I did this so that she would release my arm and so that I could create distance between us. I never intended to cause any harm.
7. I deny pushing Mrs Doyle with force or without provocation. At the time, I believed that she was going to hit me or continue grabbing me. I acted to defend myself. Pushing her was a natural instinct and reaction to her behaviour.
8. I understand that it is alleged that I was the aggressor. This is not true. There were witnesses who saw Mrs Doyle shouting at me and acting aggressively. I think there are some who saw her grab my arm.
9. Some witnesses are saying that I pushed her without any reason. I do not accept this. Those witnesses must have arrived after Mrs Doyle shouted at me and grabbed my arm.

10. I did not intend Mrs Doyle to fall over or sustain any injuries. I did not foresee that a simple defensive push would cause her to lose her balance. My sole intention was to protect myself from what I thought was going to be an assault.
11. I have cooperated fully with the police and have given a truthful account of what happened. I have never been in trouble before and would never assault anyone without reason.
12. I am extremely upset by all of this. I maintain that I acted in lawful self-defence, using only the force that I honestly believed was necessary at the time.

Signed: *Sarah Walker*
Date: 26 July 202#

Attachment 2

STATEMENT OF WITNESS
(Criminal Procedure Rules, r 16.2; Criminal Justice Act 1967, s 9)

Name: Paige Farmer
Age: Over 18

This statement, signed by me, is true to the best of my knowledge and belief and I make it knowing that if it is tendered in evidence I shall be liable to prosecution if I have wilfully stated in it anything which I know to be false or do not believe to be true.

I am Paige Farmer.

I was at the children's playground on 24 July 202# and observed an incident involving two women who I now know to be Mrs Sarah WALKER and Mrs Amanda Doyle. I saw Mrs Doyle approach Mrs WALKER in a very aggressive manner, shouting and waving her arms.

Mrs Doyle grabbed Mrs WALKER's arm and got very close to her face. Mrs WALKER looked startled and instinctively pushed Mrs Doyle away to protect herself. The push was brief and didn't look hard. Mrs Doyle fell to the ground and Mrs WALKER looked shocked.

I did not hear everything that was said between them, and I cannot say what happened leading up to the incident as I was busy looking after my children. From what I did see, it appeared that emotions were heightened on both sides, but Mrs Doyle made contact with Mrs Walker first.

I can only describe what I personally saw during the incident. It seems like Mrs Walker's actions were justified but I couldn't say that with any certainty, and I do not wish to make an opinion on either parties' intent.

Signed: *Paige Farmer*
Date: 26 July 202#

Attachment 3

STATEMENT OF WITNESS
(Criminal Procedure Rules, r 16.2; Criminal Justice Act 1967, s 9)

Name: Henry Harden
Age: Over 18

This statement, signed by me, is true to the best of my knowledge and belief and I make it knowing that if it is tendered in evidence I shall be liable to prosecution if I have wilfully stated in it anything which I know to be false or do not believe to be true.

I am Henry Harden.

I was at the playground on 24 July 202# and saw Mrs WALKER and Mrs Doyle near the swings. I didn't hear any noise other than the children playing. I looked over as my children wanted to play on the swings, and saw Mrs WALKER suddenly push Mrs Doyle with significant force.

Mrs Doyle fell and hit her face on the ground. Mrs Doyle didn't touch or threaten Mrs WALKER beforehand. The push seemed deliberate and disproportionate. I am concerned that Mrs WALKER used excessive force.

Signed: *Henry Harden*
Date: 26 July 202#

Attachment 4

IN THE NOTTINGHAM MAGISTRATES' COURT

BETWEEN:

[insert]

-v-

[insert]

DEFENCE STATEMENT

---

1. This Defence Statement is served pursuant to s 6A of the Criminal Procedure and Investigations Act 1996. It is made without prejudice to assist the Crown in identifying relevant matters for the purposes of disclosure.
2. All references are to the Criminal Procedure and Investigations Act 1996 unless otherwise stated.

This statement sets out in general terms my defence to the allegations contained within the indictment. I understand that in signing it I accept all responsibility for its accuracy. I instruct that my solicitors serve it on my behalf.

Signed:
Date:

* * *

■ YOUR TURN

Have a go at answering question 1, remembering the guidance on page 86.

- Use a structured approach as required by the SRA's assessment criteria on page 87.
- Be professional and comply with legal principles.
- Ensure that you are legally and factually accurate, and identify the elements of the offence.
- Identify any ethical or professional conduct issues that arise.
- Timings are important: you will need to prepare and write your answer in 45 minutes. Be mindful of how long you want to spend preparing, writing and reviewing your answer.

SQE1 Functioning legal knowledge link

The general principles of criminal law were considered in chapter 1 of ***Revise SQE: Criminal Law***. In chapters 4 and 6, we focused on the offence of ABH and the defence of self-defence. Remember that in constructing your defence statement you need to identify which elements of the offence you accept and which you deny. As part of this, you will need to know how those elements are defined and what the prosecution must prove. Be clear as to why you say the defence of self-defence is made out, and review your understanding of these two topics before you proceed.

EVALUATING YOUR ANSWER

When you have attempted question 1, mark it yourself against the SQE2 legal drafting assessment criteria. Do you think your attempt met the threshold standard?

Now compare your attempt with the following key legal points and two sample answers to the question. A circled number indicates that commentary is provided for this part of the answer. The commentary explains whether or not the sample answer satisfies the assessment criteria and is likely to meet the SQE2 threshold standard.

➥Key legal points: question 1

- Note that, while citations are generally not required, s 47 of the Offences Against the Person Act 1861 is a listed authority in the SQE2 assessment specification, so you may be expected to recite or recall that section as part of your defence statement.
- The key question here is whether Mrs Walker's actions amount to ABH contrary to s 47 Offences Against the Person Act 1861, or whether her actions were in lawful self-defence.
- The defence statement should set out what issues the defence takes with the offence of ABH and what they say about self-defence.
- From the facts given, it is agreed that Mrs Doyle suffered a minor concussion and visible bruising. This is likely to amount to an ABH offence; therefore, the question is whether Mrs Walker's use of force was 'lawful'. The defence statement should clearly set out that Mrs Walker accepts causing the injury with intent. The identifying point is whether she has a defence under common law principles of self-defence.
- Here, Mrs Walker claims that she was approached, verbally abused and grabbed by Mrs Doyle. Mrs Walker says that she only pushed Mrs Doyle because of this, and did so instinctively to protect herself. If this is believed, then her position that she used necessary force is supported. The question therefore becomes whether force was reasonable in the circumstances.
- The fact that Mrs Doyle suffered injury does not in and of itself make the force excessive. If the push was particularly forceful or disproportionate, the court may find it to be beyond what was necessary.

- There are additional considerations. The question says that there were witnesses but their accounts vary. The prosecution will argue that the push was unjustified and/or excessive. The defence statement should set out the basis of the self-defence, the facts and the defence's views on the prosecution witnesses.
- Deal with all aspects of the defence statement as instructed, save for alibi (which is irrelevant) and points of law (there are none).
- As with all legal drafting, the statement must be concise, accurate and professionally drafted. Failure to serve a defence statement may result in adverse inferences being drawn at trial if there is something later relied upon by the defence. The defence statement must therefore clearly reflect Mrs Walker's account.

■ SAMPLE ANSWER 1 TO QUESTION 1

IN THE NOTTINGHAM MAGISTRATES' COURT

BETWEEN

REX

-v-

SARAH WALKER

DEFENCE STATEMENT

---

1. This Defence Statement is served pursuant to s 6A of the Criminal Procedure and Investigations Act 1996. It is made without prejudice to assist the Crown in identifying relevant matters for the purposes of disclosure.
2. All references are to the Criminal Procedure and Investigations Act 1996 unless otherwise stated.
3. The defendant faces trial for one charge of Assault Occasioning Actual Bodily Harm contrary to s 47 Offences Against the Person Act 1861. This defence statement pertains to that offence alone. ❶
4. The defendant expressly reserves her right to decide whether or not to give evidence. Anything said in this Defence Statement which may conflict with that principle is to be interpreted as being thereby qualified. ❷

The nature of the defence

5. In advancing her defence the defendant will say:
   i. She was approached by the complainant in an aggressive manner without provocation.
   ii. The complainant was shouting and grabbed the defendant's arm, causing her to feel threatened.
   iii. The defendant believed she was about to be assaulted and acted instinctively to protect herself. The defendant acted in lawful self-defence.
   iv. The push was proportionate to the imminent threat and the defendant did not intend to cause injury.
   v. She had no intent to commit unlawful violence and was motivated purely by a fear for her own safety. ❸

The matters of fact with which the defendant takes issue

6. The defendant denies the following:
   i. That the defendant acted unlawfully.
   ii. That the force used was excessive or disproportionate.

   iii. That the complainant's injuries were caused by an unlawful assault rather than an instinctive defensive action.

7. The defendant takes issue with the prosecution about these matters for the following reasons:
   i. She will say that the complainant was verbally abusive towards her and grabbed hold of her arm.
   ii. She will say that the complainant was screaming and got close to her face.
   iii. She does not deny pushing the complainant.
   iv. She accepts that there was a confrontation but that she felt that she had to protect herself.
   v. She did not commit the offences alleged. ❹

Points of law

8. The defendant requires the prosecution to comply with the relevant Criminal Procedure Rules relating to bad character and hearsay evidence, and notes that no application has been lodged seeking the admission of any such material. ❺

Witnesses to be called by the defendant

9. The prosecution intends to rely on evidence from Mrs Amanda Doyle and Mr Henry Harden.
10. The defendant does not at this stage of proceedings intend to rely upon any witnesses. Should this position change, she will serve a supplement to this Statement setting out any details of any witnesses she intends to rely upon. ❻

Initial disclosure

11. The defence requests disclosure of the following material, in accordance with the Crown's continuing obligation:
   i. Up-to-date antecedents of all Crown witnesses.
   ii. All photographs, CCTV, relevant witness statements of the incident of scene, the defendant and the complainant.
12. The above matters are sought as continuing disclosure (in addition to the below) if it is considered they do not fall within the Act.

Continuing disclosure

13. Furthermore, the defence requests disclosure of the following items in accordance with the Crown's obligations in respect of disclosure:
   i. Copies of all unused statements.
   ii. Copies of all incident logs and crime reports pertaining to this investigation.

   The defence further requests any other material not hitherto disclosed that might reasonably be expected to assist the defence or undermine the case for the Crown. ❼

This statement sets out in general terms my defence to the allegations contained within the indictment. I understand that in signing it I accept all responsibility for its accuracy. I instruct that my solicitors serve it on my behalf.

Signed:
Date:

COMMENTARY

1. The candidate clearly and accurately identifies the offence that the defendant is alleged to have committed. Reference to the relevant offence is precise and appropriately limits the statement to just that offence, satisfying the SQE2 assessment criterion for accuracy.
2. This statement is included to protect the defendant's right not to incriminate themselves. This allows them to keep their position flexible as the case develops. While the wording ensures that the defence is protected, it is not essential in all defence statements.
3. Using subheadings for each section of this defence statement allows the reader (or assessor) to identify whether each criterion has been met. Lists and sublists help to make the information more accessible, and would assist the prosecution, court and advocates in identifying the items in dispute.
4. This section goes beyond denials and sets out the defence account, which directly challenges the prosecution case. The structure is logical and sets out the denials with reasoning, which is a good skill to develop in legal drafting. The client's instructions are conveyed and implemented in a clear manner.
5. The inclusion of a section on points of law correctly anticipates the procedural issues which may arise and reflects forward-thinking case management, a skill that runs through the heart of the SQE2. Pre-empting a situation such as this shows a solid understanding of the litigation process.
6. Although no defence witnesses are named, the candidate clearly identifies the ongoing right to include witnesses should any arise. This reflects the instructions given: the candidate is told that there were witnesses to the incident, but no details are given that could identify them, nor is the candidate told that the defence will rely upon them.
7. The disclosure requests are appropriately detailed and clearly distinguish initial and continuing disclosure. This demonstrates a good practical application of legal rules and real-world applicability.

Does this answer meet the threshold?

This answer likely meets the assessment passing threshold. The drafting is clear, accurate and logically structured: it clearly identifies and applies the correct statutory frameworks, structures the content around each required component and uses subheadings to enhance the clarity of the statement.

The material facts of the case are integrated well, without forming a sea of text that loses coherence. Drafting in this way makes good use of the instructions given to the candidate because each element is set out without going into too much detail. This shows an ability to extract information and apply it to written legal documents. The information is set out in such a way that assists the parties and the court in understanding the defence and compliance with rules and procedures. In the context of the SQE2 assessment, it helps the assessor to identify key points and decide whether the assessment criteria have been met.

There are no critical misunderstandings in this defence statement and the drafting shows a clear and professional standard of communication throughout. There are parts that are repetitive or could have been developed further, but they do not have major implications for the pass standard.

Now consider the second sample answer to question 1.

■ SAMPLE ANSWER 2 TO QUESTION 1

IN THE NOTTINGHAM MAGISTRATES' COURT

BETWEEN

REX

-v-

MRS SARAH WALKER

DEFENCE STATEMENT

---

1. This Defence Statement is served pursuant to s 6A of the Criminal Procedure and Investigations Act 1996. It is made without prejudice to assist the Crown in identifying relevant matters for the purposes of disclosure.
2. All references are to the Criminal Procedure and Investigations Act 1996 unless otherwise stated.
3. This defence statement is provided in relation to the charge of Assault Occasioning Actual Bodily Harm. The defendant denies the allegation made by the complainant. ❶

Nature of the defence

4. The defendant says that the complainant was being abusive towards her and was very aggressive, causing her to fear for her safety. The defendant does not remember exactly what was said but says that she was scared.
5. The defendant says that she may have pushed the complainant, but she didn't mean to hurt her and didn't think it would result in injury. ❷

Matters in issue

6. The defendant dispute that she acts unlawfully or with intent to cause harm. She accepts that there was physical contact but denies committing the offence. ❸

Witnesses

7. The defendant acknowledges that there were people nearby who witnessed the incident.
8. At this stage the defence does not intend to rely on any witnesses but if this changes the court and prosecution will be informed. ❹

Disclosure

9. The defendant would like to see any CCTV, photographs and any other evidence that the prosecution has. The defendant also requests any information about the complainant and their background. ❺

This statement sets out in general terms my defence to the allegations contained within the indictment. I understand that in signing it I accept all responsibility for its accuracy. I instruct that my solicitors serve it on my behalf.

Signed:
Date:

COMMENTARY

1. The candidate identifies the offence and includes a bare denial. This point could be improved by giving reference to the statutory provision with which the offence is made out (s 47 Offences Against the Person Act 1861). The language used is vague in part, and does not make specific reference to the allegation made. This could make it unclear to the court (in this case the SQE2 assessor) what the precise issues in dispute are, and whether the defendant intends to formally enter a plea despite indicating that they deny guilt.
2. A good use of appropriate headings makes the defence statement easy to read and understand. It allows the assessor to identify the elements of the question that have been dealt with. Remember the requirements of the assessment criteria to use clear, precise, concise and acceptable language: this draft only partially achieves this: (1) at times, the language in this response is informal - 'being abusive' and 'very aggressive' are general, passing statements and do not set out the specific nature of the offence; (2) the use of contractions (ie 'didn't') is inappropriate for legal drafting; (3) the elements required to rely on self-defence are not identified clearly.
3. This section identifies that the allegation is denied but it does not clearly specify which elements are denied. The document needs to be legally comprehensive in order to meet the assessment criteria. There is an evident spelling mistake of 'dispute' instead of 'disputes', and a tense error in 'acts' which should be 'acted'. Remember to review your draft carefully for these types of error.
4. This section steers towards the witnesses, hinting that some may be called but lacking precision. Referring to people being nearby is vague and does not identify their position with regard to the alleged offence. The candidate's statement that the court and prosecution will be informed if any witnesses are to be called is correct, but this could have been achieved in a more cohesive and professional manner (see sample answer 1 to question 1, paragraph 10, which is more successful here).
5. The disclosure element demonstrates an understanding of the requirements of the defence statement but is not executed well. As it stands, this section is vague and quite informal. It would benefit from being more specific and focused to the case at hand.

Does this answer meet the threshold?

This draft likely does not meet the pass threshold. It is structured well and makes good use of headings and clear language in general, which will assist the assessor. However, it is too brief and does not demonstrate the required proficiency.

The answer does not make use of the relevant legal principles and fails to appropriately apply them to the case. A more developed answer could have produced a much more cohesive defence statement and thereby met the assessment criteria. In sample answer 2, the issues in dispute are not properly identified or explained, which makes the draft less effective. More detail and precision in each section could have pushed it into the higher competence band. Finally, the lack of formality and minor inconsistencies could undermine the professionalism expected of a legal draft of this level to meet the threshold.

Below is an example of how another part of the specification could be assessed in the context of legal drafting on SQE2 - admissibility/exclusion of evidence. This question applies the knowledge that you will have gained from chapter 6 of ***Revise SQE: Criminal Practice***.

■ QUESTION 2

Email to candidate

From: Partner
Sent: 20 August 202#
To: Candidate
Subject: Sections 76 and 78 PACE 1984, Application to exclude evidence

We have a new matter that requires your assistance. Our client is Mr Kareem Lewis, and he is due to appear before Sheffield Magistrates' Court for trial in the next few months. He instructed us after being charged with fraud by false representation. He did not have a solicitor in his police interview and there are now concerns over an alleged confession he made during that interview.

The admissibility of our client's confession may be subject to challenge due to a potential breach of the Police and Criminal Evidence Act (PACE) 1984 and the Codes of Practice during police interview. As such, an application under s 78 PACE to exclude the evidence is likely to be necessary in the circumstances. In addition, you should consider whether the alleged confession meets the requirements of s 76 PACE 1984, whereby a confession is inadmissible if it is obtained through oppression or in other circumstances that would render it unreliable.

You are tasked with drafting the skeleton argument for this application using the template provided (Attachment 4). Note to candidates: both s 76 and s 78 should be addressed.

All necessary information is attached, including Mr Lewis's proof of evidence (Attachment 1) and the witness statement of PC Oliver Graham (Attachment 2). Below is a list of the relevant authorities with a brief note about their relevance, should you wish to include them in the skeleton argument:

- ss 76 and 78 PACE 1984 (see Attachment 3)
- Code C, PACE Codes of Practice – 6.4, 6.5, 6.6, 11.5, 11.7, 11.8
- *R v Walsh* [1990] 91 Cr App R 161 – held that significant and substantial breaches of PACE and Codes of Practice could justify exclusion of evidence under s 78
- *R v Canale* [1990] 2 All ER 187 – held that confession evidence may be excluded where an interview is not properly recorded or written up later in breach of Code C PACE.

Many thanks,

Partner

Attachments:

1. Proof of evidence of Mr Kareem Lewis
2. Witness statement of PC Oliver Graham
3. Extracts from ss 76 and 78 PACE 1984
4. Skeleton argument template

Attachment 1

PROOF OF EVIDENCE OF MR KAREEM LEWIS

KAREEM LEWIS WILL SAY:

1. I live at 3 Devonshire Walk, Sheffield. I am 21 years of age and intend to plead NOT GUILTY to the charge of fraud by false representation.
2. On 30/07/202#, at around 11.45 P.M., I was stopped by police officers and subject to a search. They informed me that I was suspected of using another person's bank card to make fraudulent purchases. I was searched and the police officers took a bank card from my pocket, some receipts and around £1,500 in cash.
3. I was arrested at the scene and taken to the police station for an interview, which took place at 2.15 A.M.
4. I kept asking for legal representation before and during the interview but I did not receive this. The custody officer did not attempt to contact the duty solicitor until after the interview had concluded. At no stage during the interview was a solicitor present, despite my repeated requests.
5. During the interview, I repeatedly asked for it to be stopped for various reasons. I did not want to continue without my solicitor present. I was distressed by the nature of the questions being asked. I was also tired and fatigued, having not eaten for several hours before my arrest. I found it difficult to focus on what was being said and asked of me.
6. I was told several times during the interview by the officer that the sooner I answered their questions, the sooner they would give me some food and allow me to sleep. Throughout the interview, the officers also suggested that if I confessed and admitted to using the card then I would get a lighter sentence. They continued to question me even though I made it clear that I wanted to stop.
7. It is alleged that I admitted to making fraudulent transactions during the interview. I deny this and any possible admission made was not voluntary.
8. The interview was not audio- or video-recorded, and no notes were taken. The following day, one of the interviewing officers wrote some notes from his memory, which I believe are inaccurate and contain several mistakes.
9. I have raised concerns about how the interview was conducted several times, but have been told by the same interviewing officer that everything was done properly. I do not agree with this.
10. I am concerned about the reliability and voluntariness of any alleged confession and the implications of this. The admission of such evidence would compromise the fairness of the ongoing proceedings.

Signed: *Kareem Lewis*
Date: 10 August 202#

Attachment 2

STATEMENT OF WITNESS

(Criminal Procedure Rules, r 16.2; Criminal Justice Act 1967, s 9)

Name: PC 7359 Oliver Graham
Age: Over 18

This statement, signed by me, is true to the best of my knowledge and belief and I make it knowing that if it is tendered in evidence I shall be liable to prosecution if I have wilfully stated in it anything which I know to be false or do not believe to be true.

My name is Oliver Graham, and I am a police officer with the Sheffield Police Force. I have been employed in this role since 2021. I make this statement in relation to the interview of Mr Kareem Lewis conducted by me on 31/07/202#.

Mr Lewis was arrested on suspicion of fraud by false representation. He was informed of the reason for his arrest and his rights under PACE including the right to legal representation. Mr Lewis indicated that he did not wish to have a solicitor present during the interview. I ensured that he understood this right and his decision to proceed was voluntary.

I introduced myself and explained the purpose of the interview. I conducted the interview in a professional and non-coercive manner. At no point did I threaten, intimidate or use oppressive techniques to obtain a confession.

During the interview, Mr Lewis made certain admissions relating to the alleged offence. No notes were taken during the interview, but these admissions were noted in full the following day.

I believe that any statements made by Mr Lewis were voluntary and there was no use of oppression or inducement.

Signed: *Oliver Graham*
Date: 2 August 202#

Attachment 3

Police and Criminal Evidence Act (PACE) 1984

76 Confessions

(1) In any proceedings a confession made by an accused person may be given in evidence against him in so far as it is relevant to any matter in issue in the proceedings and is not excluded by the court in pursuance of this section.
(2) If, in any proceedings where the prosecution proposes to give in evidence a confession made by an accused person, it is represented to the court that the confession was or may have been obtained—
  (a) by oppression of the person who made it; or
  (b) in consequence of anything said or done which was likely, in the circumstances existing at the time, to render unreliable any confession which might be made by him in consequence thereof,

the court shall not allow the confession to be given in evidence against him except in so far as the prosecution proves to the court beyond reasonable doubt that the confession (notwithstanding that it may be true) was not obtained as aforesaid.

...

(8) In this section 'oppression' includes torture, inhuman or degrading treatment, and the use or threat of violence (whether or not amounting to torture).

78 Exclusion of unfair evidence

(1) In any proceedings the court may refuse to allow evidence on which the prosecution proposes to rely to be given if it appears to the court that, having regard to all the circumstances, including the circumstances in which the evidence was obtained, the admission of the evidence would have such an adverse effect on the fairness of the proceedings that the court ought not to admit it.

(2) Nothing in this section shall prejudice any rule of law requiring a court to exclude evidence.

Attachment 4

IN THE [insert name of court]

BETWEEN:

[insert]

-v-

[insert]

SKELETON ARGUMENT ON BEHALF OF [INSERT NAME]

---

* * *

■ YOUR TURN

Have a go at answering question 2, remembering the guidance on page 86.

- Use a structured approach as required by the SRA's assessment criteria on page 87.
- Be professional and comply with legal principles.
- Ensure that you are legally and factually accurate, and identify the elements of the offence.
- Identify any ethical or professional conduct issues that arise.
- Timings are important: you will need to prepare and write your answer in 45 minutes. Be mindful of how long you want to spend preparing, writing and reviewing your answer.

SQE1 Functioning legal knowledge link

In chapters 1 and 6 of ***Revise SQE: Criminal Practice***, we dealt with the issues of police interviews, including the conduct of police during interviews, the rights of suspects under interview and the possible consequences following breach of any PACE Codes of Practice. We also discussed the law relating to the exclusion of confessions under s 76 PACE 1984 and the discretionary power to exclude prosecution evidence under s 78 PACE 1984. Ensure you review your functioning legal knowledge on these two topics before you proceed.

EVALUATING YOUR ANSWER

When you have attempted question 2, mark it yourself against the SQE2 legal drafting assessment criteria. Do you think your attempt met the threshold standard?

Now compare your attempt with the following key legal points and two sample answers to the question. A circled number indicates that commentary is provided for this part of the answer. The commentary explains whether or not the sample answer satisfies the assessment criteria and is likely to meet the SQE2 threshold standard.

➥Key legal points: question 2

- The question requires you to consider whether the admission of the confession would have an adverse effect on the fairness of proceedings such that it ought to be excluded. The skeleton argument that you are tasked with drafting should be framed around the statutory interpretation and apply a clear test derived from statute and case law given.
- You will know from SQE1 that s 78 PACE gives the court discretion to exclude prosecution evidence. Code C PACE outlines how suspects should be treated, including their rights to legal advice, interviews, rest and conditions. In this case, the elements to be analysed are:
  1. Was there a significant or substantial breach of Code C?
  2. Does that breach have an adverse effect on the fairness of proceedings?
  3. Was the confession reliable and voluntary under the conditions?
- You are given case law, which may assist with writing your submissions to the court. It will be more persuasive if you attempt to link statute or case law to each breach or point.
- Mr Lewis was denied access to a solicitor before his interview; the fact pattern tells the candidate that he repeatedly asked for a solicitor but the custody officer failed to put this into motion. Under Code C PACE, once a detainee requests legal advice, the interview should be delayed until a solicitor has been provided - except for exceptional circumstances. There is no evidence here of exceptional circumstances for proceeding without a solicitor, and this could constitute a breach of Mr Lewis's rights. *R v Walsh* had similar facts where a breach justified the exclusion of evidence.
- Mr Lewis had not eaten and was visibly distressed during his interview, which took place in the early hours of the morning. Detainees should be given adequate rest and food. Conducting an interview where the detainee does not understand the proceedings and is fatigued casts doubt on the reliability of any statement that Mr Lewis gave (Code C PACE, paragraph 3).
- Interviewing officers told Mr Lewis that, if he answered questions and confessed, he would get a lighter sentence, and the food and sleep that he wanted. A confession *must* be voluntary. Threats, promises and inducement can render any confession inadmissible. There is a potential for the confession to be given under oppression (s 76(2)(a) PACE).
- The interview was not recorded, and no notes were made at the time or shortly after the interview. Code C requires interviews to be properly recorded. This was further reinforced in *R v Canale*, where interviews were not recorded and the confession was excluded.
- You should argue how a culmination of breaches will undermine the fairness of proceedings, especially as a confession would be central to the evidence and the charge.

■ SAMPLE ANSWER 1 TO QUESTION 2

IN THE SHEFFIELD MAGISTRATES' COURT

BETWEEN

REX

-v-

KAREEM LEWIS

SKELETON ARGUMENT ON BEHALF OF KAREEM LEWIS

Introduction

1. This is a defence application pursuant to s 76 and s 78 Police and Criminal Evidence Act (PACE) 1984 to exclude evidence of an alleged confession made by the defendant, Mr LEWIS, during a police interview conducted on 31/07/202#.
2. The defence submits that the confession was obtained in breach of the defendant's rights under PACE and associated Codes of Practice. The evidence ought to be excluded either because:
   a) Under s 76, the confession was obtained by oppression or is rendered unreliable by the circumstances in which it was made and must not be admitted; or alternatively
   b) Under s 78, its admission would have such adverse effect on the fairness of proceedings that the court ought to exclude it. ❶

Factual background ❷

3. The defendant was arrested at approximately 11.45 P.M. on 30/07/202# on suspicion of fraud by false representation. He was taken to the police station and interviewed shortly after 02.15 A.M.
4. The defendant states that during the interview:
   a) The defendant requested legal representation, but the duty solicitor was not contacted until after the interview had concluded.
   b) The defendant was clearly distressed and confused, and asked to stop the interview on several occasions.
   c) The interviewing officers made several improper inducements and suggested to the defendant that he would 'get a lighter sentence' if he confessed.
   d) Mr Lewis allegedly made a confession that he had used the bank card that was not in his name.
   e) The interview was not recorded via audio or video recordings, and any notes were made several hours later and were inconsistent. ❸

Legal framework

5. Under s 76(2) PACE the court must exclude a defendant's confession if it may have been obtained through oppression or in circumstances that make it unreliable. It is for the prosecution to prove beyond reasonable doubt that no impropriety occurred.
6. Section 78(1) PACE states that the court can refuse to allow evidence if it appears that the circumstances in which it was obtained would have such an adverse effect on the fairness of the proceedings that the court should not admit it.
7. Under Code C, interviewers must not use oppression to obtain answers or a statement. They should not make suggestions about what will happen if the

person answers unless the interviewee specifically asks. Every interview should also be recorded. The only exception for not having records of the interview is if it would be impractical or disruptive to do so.

8. The court has a discretion to exclude evidence where there have been significant and substantial breaches of PACE or the PACE Codes of Conduct, per *R v Walsh* [1990] 91 Cr App R 161. ❹

Submissions
Under s 76(2)

9. The defence submits that any confession made as alleged is inadmissible under s 76(2) because Mr Lewis was denied access to legal advice despite his repeated requests. He was subject to interview whilst visibly distressed, exhausted and without food, and continued to be questioned despite asking for the interview to be stopped.
10. Moreover, the confession that Mr Lewis is alleged to have made was done so as a result of inducements made by the interviewing officers, who said that he would receive a lighter sentence if he were to confess, as well as them offering to give him food if he confessed. In the state that Mr Lewis found himself in, any confession should be rendered unreliable.

In the alternative:
Under s 78

11. Even if the confession is not excluded under s 76, the defence submits that it should be excluded under s 78 because it would have such an adverse effect on the fairness of proceedings that the court ought not to admit it.

    The following breaches of PACE and Codes of Practice are relied upon:

    a) Mr Lewis repeatedly requested legal representation before and during the interview, but the custody officer failed to contact the duty solicitor until after the interview concluded. Denying him of legal advice/representation is a clear breach of Code C which provides that a detainee must be informed of and allowed to consult a solicitor at any time.
    b) Interviewing officers told Mr Lewis that he would receive food and a lighter sentence if he confessed. The statements mentioned amount to improper inducements and may constitute oppression under s 76(2)(b) PACE. Furthermore, Code C prohibits officers from attempting to obtain answers through oppression.
    c) The interview was not audio- or video-recorded, and no notes were written. A written record was made the following day by one of the officers, but it contained several inaccuracies. This is another breach of Code C, which requires contemporaneous record to be kept (*R v Canale* [1990] 2 All ER 187). ❺

Conclusion

12. In light of the above, the defence respectfully submits that the confession is unreliable and/or, in the alternative, its admission would compromise the fairness of proceedings. The court is invited to exclude the confession pursuant to s 76 PACE or exercise its discretion under s 78 PACE and exclude the confession from the evidence. ❻

COMMENTARY

1. The introduction succinctly outlines the basis for an application under ss 76 and 78 PACE. It immediately identifies the grounds for the application and frames the position for the assessor. This shows an accurate identification of the legal issues in this case and the purpose is stated clearly.
2. The document is well structured, using headings for the submissions that clearly set out to the assessor what they are about to read. The language used in this draft document is formal, objective and appropriate for a court document. This response satisfies the assessment criteria.
3. This section includes relevant facts, outlining the timeline, the defendant's position and the conduct of the officers. The factual background is structured logically, using a sublist of paragraphs to present the ideas effectively. This demonstrates professionalism and allows the reader to easily digest what they are reading. Each paragraph focuses on separate facts; this is best practice and demonstrates to the assessor the candidate's ability to organise information.
4. This section makes good use of the candidate's legal understanding of PACE and the importance of case law in making submissions to the court. Including the correct statutory test under PACE demonstrates a deeper understanding of legal principles, and the use of direct quotations shows a further attention to detail. The additional authority of *R v Walsh* indicates a comprehensive, well-rounded understanding of the case law that is applicable. The response meets the SQE2 assessment criteria as the drafted document is legally correct and comprehensive.
5. This section correctly identifies the key breaches: denial of legal advice, improper inducement and failure to record the interview. The candidate is demonstrating their understanding of the case and correct application of legal principles to the facts.
6. The conclusion is concise and clearly sets out the aim of the application for the court to assess. It reaffirms the fairness under s 78 PACE and ends with a professional invitation for judicial direction and request to the court.

Does this answer meet the threshold?

This skeleton argument likely meets the threshold of competence for the SQE2 legal drafting assessment because it demonstrates clear legal reasoning, appropriate structure and effective written communication. The candidate accurately identifies the legal issues and applies the law in a logical manner. The facts are relevant and focused, and the candidate summarises the defence position in a professional manner without exaggerating. The submissions show the candidate's sound judgement and understanding of how a breach may render evidence inadmissible.

The document uses the correct procedural format and has clear subheadings, which makes for a more logical and cogent piece of drafting. Language throughout the draft is professional and concise to its intended audience, with correct and appropriate use of legal terminology. The conclusion summarises the relief sought in a respectful and persuasive tone. The tone is suitable for a Crown Court application and shows a high standard of legal communication.

Now consider the second sample answer to question 2.

SAMPLE ANSWER 2 TO QUESTION 2

IN THE SHEFFIELD MAGISTRATES' COURT

BETWEEN

REX

-v-

MR KAREEM LEWIS

SKELETON ARGUMENT ON BEHALF OF [INSERT NAME] ❶

Introduction ❷

This is a defence application under s 78 PACE to exclude a confession made by the defendant during a police interview. The defence submits that the confession was obtained unfairly and in breach of the defendant's rights under PACE and the Codes of Practise and that its admission would adversely affect the fairness of proceedings. ❸

Factual background

Mr Lewis was arrested at around 11.45 P.M. on suspicion of fraud by false representation. He was taken to the police station and interviewed at approximately 2.15 A.M. During the interview, he asked for a solicitor several times, but the duty solicitor was not contacted until after the interview ended. Mr Lewi was tired and had not eaten. He asked to stop the interview but was told by officers that if he answered questions, he would get food and sleep. He was also told that if he admitted to using the bank card that was not registered in his name, he would get a lighter sentence. The interview was not recorded, and notes were made the next day, which were not accurate. ❹

Legal framework

Section 78(1) PACE allows the court to exclude evidence. Code C of the PACE Codes of Practise sets out the rules for interviews, including the right to legal advice and the requirement to avoid oppression. The interview should also be recorded properly. ❺

Submissions

The defence submits that the confession should be excluded because of the following:

- Mr Lewis was denied legal advice, which is a breach of Code C.
- The officers made comments that could be seen as inducements, which may amount to oppression.
- The interview was not recorded, and the notes made later were inaccurate.

These issues show that the confession was not obtained fairly and should not be used in court. ❻

Conclusion

The defence asks the court to exclude the confession under s 78 PACE because of the unfair way it was obtained. ❼

COMMENTARY

1. The heading is immediately incorrect as the candidate has failed to include the relevant name in the header of the skeleton argument. This is a key factor, first when directing the reader/court to the relevant document and second for clarity and precision.
2. It is important to note from the outset the poor structure that has been adopted in this answer. Although headings have been correctly and usefully included, the absence of paragraph numbers makes it difficult to follow and understand the points being made. Try to make your draft as clear as possible: numbered paragraphs allow the reader to navigate the text easily, and should always be adopted as a fundamental aspect of drafting a legal document.
3. The introduction identifies the statutory basis for the application, which is a positive start, but it lacks precision and depth. Furthermore, the skeleton argument completely ignores s 76, which is a vital aspect of the submission. The skeleton argument should cite the full provision of PACE – spelled out as the Police and Criminal Evidence Act 1984 – or at the very least identify the provision in detail. The spelling mistake of 'Practise' as opposed to 'Practice' is not particularly fatal, but does demonstrate the candidate's need to thoroughly check spelling and grammar when reviewing their answer.
4. The factual background is also relevant but underdeveloped. It outlines the sequence of events but lacks clarity and structure. In parts, the language is informal and lacks specificity. There is a spelling mistake of the defendant's name ('Lewi' for 'Lewis'), which again demonstrates a lack of attention to detail and means that the legal draft is not comprehensive.
5. The legal framework needs work here; it is brief and lacks authority. Mentioning s 78 and Code C is a step in the right direction, but the skeleton argument fails to quote, paraphrase or direct to the appropriate statutory test or any case law that could be relevant. Furthermore, as mentioned above, s 76 is entirely missed by the candidate. This weakens the foundation of the argument and suggests a limited understanding of the relevant law, indicating that the candidate will not satisfy the assessment criteria.
6. The submissions clearly identify three key issues but do so in a vague and unstructured manner so that the submission lacks power and confidence. The candidate could have analysed how each breach affected the fairness of proceedings, to assist the court and the assessor in understanding why the submissions are being made. Citing the supporting case law or statutory authority would strengthen the submissions, and linking them to the legal framework section would create a more cohesive draft.
7. The conclusion restates the application and makes clear what is wanted, but it does not give a reason why the court should exclude the evidence or explain their impact. A stronger conclusion would reinforce the test and seriousness of the procedural failure, thus making it more persuasive.

Does this answer meet the threshold?

This skeleton argument likely does not meet the threshold for the assessment. While it shows awareness of the legal issues and structure, this response lacks the depth and analysis required. First, the legal reasoning is underdeveloped: references to s 78 and Code C of PACE are well made, but the candidate does not reference case law that was provided by the instructions and is essential to the argument. Furthermore, this answer does not address s 76 of PACE as the instructions directly ask candidates to do, which would be a fatal omission in this piece of drafting. Second, the language is vague and lacks precision. At times the argument is speculative, lacks detail and does not demonstrate a clear and confident legal analysis translated into the drafting. Third, the account of the factual background, while relevant, is informal and unstructured, which makes it difficult for the court or assessor to follow. Overall, the drafting lacks the depth, clarity and professional tone required to meet the SQE2 standard threshold.

■ KEY POINT CHECKLIST

This chapter has covered the following key knowledge points:

- The SQE2 assessment criteria for legal drafting and how to apply them in the context of criminal litigation.
- A suggested structure for approaching an SQE2 legal drafting question in criminal litigation.
- Examples of legal drafting responses that are either likely or unlikely to meet the threshold standard, with full commentary on their strengths and weaknesses.

■ SUMMARY AND REFLECTION

Your drafting task will begin with an email from a partner that provides you with the context and the question that you must answer. Your obligation is to respond directly to what is being asked. Try to avoid digression and general commentary about what is being drafted, and instead focus on applying legal principles to the facts of the case.

Your writing should be clear, concise and purposeful. Every word should be necessary, so do not write in an elaborate, academic manner - you are tasked with drafting writing a legal document, not an essay. Create a structure for your document that makes the information you are trying to convey easy to understand and absorb. Think about how *you* would understand the content if you were receiving this document. A well-structured answer not only helps your reader or assessor to follow your argument but also showcases your organisational skills and legal reasoning.

FINAL WORDS

We hope that the guidance and examples contained in this book have helped to put into context how to use your practice skills to ensure you reach the SQE2 grading criteria. Remember, above all, that this is an assessment, and the assessor needs to see evidence that you have met the criteria in order for you to pass the threshold. Always keep this in the back of your mind when taking your SQE2 assessments.

While this book is designed to aid your learning and provide helpful tips on how to pass your SQE2 assessments, it is no substitute for practice. All skills are improved with repetition and refining your technique, and legal skills are no exception to this rule. Take any opportunity you can to write letters, draft legal documents and practise your interviewing and advocacy skills. Reflect carefully on your performance after each exercise:

- What could you have done better?
- Did you meet all of the grading criteria applicable to that particular skill?
- Do you need to fill any gaps in your legal knowledge?

Constant practice and self-reflection are the keys to success.

Finally, the team at *Revise SQE* wish you the best of luck in your SQE2 assessments!

Appendix

PERFORMANCE INDICATORS FOR SQE2
CASE AND MATTER ANALYSIS ASSESSMENT CRITERIA

Skills	*Indicators demonstrating competence*	*Indicators that do not demonstrate competence*
Identify relevant facts	• The candidate selects facts that are important in ensuring the client's needs/objectives are met, or are relevant to the legal analysis, from the documentation provided	• The candidate refers to all facts from the documentation, regardless of whether or not they are important in meeting the client's objectives or relevant to their legal analysis • The candidate refers only to irrelevant facts • The candidate does not refer to sufficient relevant facts to support the legal analysis
Provide client-focused advice (ie advice which demonstrates an understanding of the problem from the client's point of view and what the client wants to achieve, not just from a legal perspective)	• The candidate demonstrates an understanding of the client's problem from the client's perspective • The candidate addresses the client's legal problem, any relevant commercial considerations and/or the client's personal circumstances, priorities, objectives and constraints	• The candidate does not approach or appreciate the client's problem from the client's perspective • The candidate does not focus on the issues identified by the client
Use clear, precise, concise and acceptable language	• The reader understands the candidate's use of language and clarity of expression • The candidate avoids unnecessary technical terms/legal jargon	• The reader struggles to understand the candidate's use of language; the answer lacks clarity and/or is poorly expressed • The reader's understanding is adversely affected by the density, length or brevity of the answer • The candidate uses unnecessary technical terms/legal jargon

Law	*Indicators demonstrating competence*	*Indicators that do not demonstrate competence*
Apply the law correctly to the client's situation	• The candidate identifies the relevant fundamental legal principles in accordance with the SQE2 assessment specification and applies them correctly to the facts of the client's case	• The candidate does not identify and correctly apply the relevant legal principles to the facts of the client's case • The candidate does not apply the relevant legal principles in a way that addresses the client's needs and concerns
Apply the law comprehensively to the client's situation	• The candidate's legal analysis is sufficiently detailed in the context of the client's case, eg assessing information to identify key issues and risks; reaching reasonable conclusions supported by relevant evidence	• The candidate's legal analysis is not sufficiently detailed in the context of the client's case, eg the candidate demonstrates little or no understanding of the key issues and risks; fails to apply the law to the facts to reach reasonable conclusions
Identify any ethical and professional conduct issues and exercise judgement to resolve them honestly and with integrity	• Where relevant, the candidate recognises ethical issues and exercises effective judgement in addressing them in accordance with the SRA Principles and rules of professional conduct	• The candidate does not recognise ethical issues or exercise effective judgement in addressing them in accordance with the SRA Principles and rules of professional conduct

PERFORMANCE INDICATORS FOR SQE2 LEGAL RESEARCH ASSESSMENT CRITERIA

Skills	*Indicators demonstrating competence*	*Indicators that do not demonstrate competence*
Identify and use relevant sources and information	• The candidate selects relevant information about the legal issue, or the client's problem, from the primary and/or secondary sources provided, eg o the candidate identifies relevant legislation/cases and/or legal explanations/ commentary in a practitioner's text, or legal encyclopaedia o the candidate extracts relevant material, such as particular provision(s) from a statute, or legal rule(s) from the Civil Procedure Rules • The candidate uses their findings to substantiate/ support their answer to the question(s) asked	• The candidate selects only irrelevant information from the primary and/or secondary sources provided • The candidate selects insufficient relevant information from the primary and/or secondary sources provided • The candidate is unable to distinguish between information that is relevant to the legal issue or the client's problem, and information that is irrelevant, eg the candidate's answer contains information drawn from all sources regardless of relevance, or from a number of irrelevant sources • The candidate does not use their findings to substantiate/ support the answer to the question(s) asked
Provide advice which is client-focused and addresses the client's problem	• The candidate demonstrates an understanding of the client's problem from the client's perspective, eg the candidate addresses the client's legal problem, any relevant commercial considerations and/or the client's priorities, objectives and constraints	• The candidate does not understand the problem from the client's perspective, eg they focus on irrelevant issues/provide advice that does not take into account the client's priorities, objectives or constraints, or is inappropriate for the client's situation
Use clear, precise, concise and acceptable language	• The candidate uses understandable and simple language to convey facts and information effectively • The candidate uses correct legal terminology where necessary	• The reader struggles to understand the candidate's use of language; the answer lacks clarity and/or is poorly expressed • The reader's understanding is adversely affected by the density or brevity of the answer • The candidate uses unnecessary or confusing technical terms/legal jargon

Law	*Indicators demonstrating competence*	*Indicators that do not demonstrate competence*
Apply the law correctly to the client's situation	• The candidate identifies the relevant legal principles and applies them correctly to the facts of the client's case	• The candidate does not identify and apply the correct legal principles to the facts of the client's case • The candidate identifies the correct legal principles but misapplies them to the client's case
Apply the law comprehensively to the client's situation	• The candidate's legal analysis is sufficiently detailed in the context of the facts of the case, eg the candidate draws on multiple sources of information to address the legal issue/client's problem effectively	• The candidate's legal analysis is not sufficiently detailed in the context of the facts of the client's case
Identify any ethical and professional conduct issues and exercise judgement to resolve them honestly and with integrity	• Where relevant, the candidate recognises ethical issues and exercises effective judgement in addressing them in accordance with the SRA Principles and rules of professional conduct	• The candidate does not recognise ethical issues or exercise effective judgement in addressing them in accordance with the SRA Principles and rules of professional conduct

PERFORMANCE INDICATORS FOR SQE2 LEGAL WRITING ASSESSMENT CRITERIA

Skills	*Indicators demonstrating competence*	*Indicators that do not demonstrate competence*
Include relevant facts	• The candidate refers to and/or addresses the salient facts provided in their instructions. Salient facts could include facts that are important in ensuring the client's needs/objectives are met, or relevant to legal advice	• The candidate includes many facts in their answer that have no bearing on their legal advice
Use a logical structure	• The candidate's presentation of information is well organised, set out clearly and easy to follow • The reader is able to understand the candidate's answer without difficulty	• The candidate's presentation of information is confused and rambling • The reader is unable to follow or understand the candidate's answer
Advice/content is client- and recipient-focused	• The candidate demonstrates an understanding of the client's circumstances including their needs, objectives and priorities • The candidate, where relevant and appropriate, explores options and advises on strategies and solutions • The candidate takes into account who the client is; recognises the key issues in the case and considers any risks • Where appropriate, the candidate imparts any difficult or unwelcome news clearly and sensitively	• The candidate does not understand the client's perspective, eg they focus on irrelevant issues/provide extraneous advice/fail to advise on relevant options, strategies and solutions • The candidate fails to take into account who the client is and does not recognise the key issues in the case or consider any risks • The candidate lacks empathy or sensitivity if imparting difficult or unwelcome news
Use clear, precise, concise and acceptable language which is appropriate to the recipient	• The reader understands the candidate's use of language and clarity of expression • The candidate's language is appropriate to the recipient and the situation • The candidate avoids unnecessary technical terms/legal jargon • The candidate uses formalities appropriate to the context and purpose of the communication	• The reader struggles to understand the candidate's use of language; the answer lacks clarity and/or is poorly expressed • The reader's understanding is adversely affected by the density or brevity of the answer • The candidate uses language that is not appropriate to the recipient and/or the situation, eg the candidate adopts an essay-style approach • The candidate uses unnecessary or confusing technical terms/legal jargon

Law	*Indicators demonstrating competence*	*Indicators that do not demonstrate competence*
Apply the law correctly to the client's situation	• The candidate identifies the correct legal principles and applies them correctly to the facts of the case	• The candidate does not identify the correct legal principles • The candidate does not apply the legal principles correctly to the client's situation
Apply the law comprehensively to the client's situation	• The candidate's writing is of sufficient detail in the context of the client's situation and the relevant factual and legal issues	• The candidate's writing is not sufficiently detailed in the context of the client's situation and the relevant factual and legal issues
Identify any ethical and professional conduct issues and exercise judgement to resolve them honestly and with integrity	• Where relevant, the candidate recognises ethical issues and exercises effective judgement in addressing them in accordance with the SRA Principles and rules of professional conduct	• The candidate does not recognise ethical issues or exercise effective judgement in addressing them in accordance with the SRA Principles and rules of professional conduct

PERFORMANCE INDICATORS FOR SQE2 LEGAL DRAFTING ASSESSMENT CRITERIA

Skills	*Indicators demonstrating competence*	*Indicators that do not demonstrate competence*
Use clear, precise, concise and acceptable language	• The candidate uses understandable and simple language to convey facts and information effectively • The candidate uses words and phrases that are suitably formal for the document being drafted • The candidate uses correct legal terminology where necessary • The document uses as few words as possible without compromising the quality of the answer	• The candidate's answer is consistently wordy, repetitive or confusing and cannot be easily understood • The meaning of the document cannot be ascertained because it contains few words • The candidate uses inappropriate language, eg the language is too informal or casual • The candidate uses unnecessary technical terms/ legal jargon throughout
Structure the document appropriately and logically	• The candidate presents facts and information in a methodical way, eg the focus, flow and direction of each paragraph is clear and appropriate signposts are used to guide the reader through the document • The way in which the candidate sets out the contents of the document achieve its purpose	• The candidate's arrangement of facts or information is disjointed or confusing, eg the paragraphing or sequencing of information is illogical • The way in which the candidate sets out the contents of the document does not achieve its purpose
Law	*Indicators demonstrating competence*	*Indicators that do not demonstrate competence*
Draft a document which is legally correct	• The candidate identifies the correct legal principles in accordance with the SQE2 assessment specification and applies them correctly in their drafting • The candidate's drafting is legally effective, eg the document contains all key information or the names of relevant parties	• The candidate does not identify the correct legal principles • The candidate does not apply the legal principles correctly in their drafting • The candidate's drafting is not legally effective
Draft a document which is legally comprehensive	• The candidate's drafting is sufficiently detailed in the context of the client's situation and the relevant factual and legal issues	• The candidate's drafting is not sufficiently detailed in the context of the client's situation and the relevant factual and legal issues
Identify any ethical and professional conduct issues and exercise judgement to resolve them honestly and with integrity	• Where relevant, the candidate recognises ethical issues and exercises effective judgement in addressing them in accordance with the SRA Principles and rules of professional conduct	• The candidate does not recognise ethical issues or exercise effective judgement in addressing them in accordance with the SRA Principles and rules of professional conduct